CS-62 GENERAL APTITUDE AND ABILITIES SERIES

This is your
PASSBOOK for...

Educating & Interacting with the Public

Test Preparation Study Guide
Questions & Answers

COPYRIGHT NOTICE

This book is SOLELY intended for, is sold ONLY to, and its use is RESTRICTED to individual, bona fide applicants or candidates who qualify by virtue of having seriously filed applications for appropriate license, certificate, professional and/or promotional advancement, higher school matriculation, scholarship, or other legitimate requirements of education and/or governmental authorities.

This book is NOT intended for use, class instruction, tutoring, training, duplication, copying, reprinting, excerption, or adaptation, etc., by:

1) Other publishers
2) Proprietors and/or Instructors of "Coaching" and/or Preparatory Courses
3) Personnel and/or Training Divisions of commercial, industrial, and governmental organizations
4) Schools, colleges, or universities and/or their departments and staffs, including teachers and other personnel
5) Testing Agencies or Bureaus
6) Study groups which seek by the purchase of a single volume to copy and/or duplicate and/or adapt this material for use by the group as a whole without having purchased individual volumes for each of the members of the group
7) Et al.

Such persons would be in violation of appropriate Federal and State statutes.

PROVISION OF LICENSING AGREEMENTS – Recognized educational, commercial, industrial, and governmental institutions and organizations, and others legitimately engaged in educational pursuits, including training, testing, and measurement activities, may address request for a licensing agreement to the copyright owners, who will determine whether, and under what conditions, including fees and charges, the materials in this book may be used them. In other words, a licensing facility exists for the legitimate use of the material in this book on other than an individual basis. However, it is asseverated and affirmed here that the material in this book CANNOT be used without the receipt of the express permission of such a licensing agreement from the Publishers. Inquiries re licensing should be addressed to the company, attention rights and permissions department.

All rights reserved, including the right of reproduction in whole or in part, in any form or by any means, electronic or mechanical, including photocopying, recording, or by any information storage and retrieval system, without permission in writing from the Publisher.

Copyright © 2024 by
National Learning Corporation

212 Michael Drive, Syosset, NY 11791
(516) 921-8888 • www.passbooks.com
E-mail: info@passbooks.com

PUBLISHED IN THE UNITED STATES OF AMERICA

PASSBOOK® SERIES

THE *PASSBOOK® SERIES* has been created to prepare applicants and candidates for the ultimate academic battlefield – the examination room.

At some time in our lives, each and every one of us may be required to take an examination – for validation, matriculation, admission, qualification, registration, certification, or licensure.

Based on the assumption that every applicant or candidate has met the basic formal educational standards, has taken the required number of courses, and read the necessary texts, the *PASSBOOK® SERIES* furnishes the one special preparation which may assure passing with confidence, instead of failing with insecurity. Examination questions – together with answers – are furnished as the basic vehicle for study so that the mysteries of the examination and its compounding difficulties may be eliminated or diminished by a sure method.

This book is meant to help you pass your examination provided that you qualify and are serious in your objective.

The entire field is reviewed through the huge store of content information which is succinctly presented through a provocative and challenging approach – the question-and-answer method.

A climate of success is established by furnishing the correct answers at the end of each test.

You soon learn to recognize types of questions, forms of questions, and patterns of questioning. You may even begin to anticipate expected outcomes.

You perceive that many questions are repeated or adapted so that you can gain acute insights, which may enable you to score many sure points.

You learn how to confront new questions, or types of questions, and to attack them confidently and work out the correct answers.

You note objectives and emphases, and recognize pitfalls and dangers, so that you may make positive educational adjustments.

Moreover, you are kept fully informed in relation to new concepts, methods, practices, and directions in the field.

You discover that you are actually taking the examination all the time: you are preparing for the examination by "taking" an examination, not by reading extraneous and/or supererogatory textbooks.

In short, this PASSBOOK®, used directedly, should be an important factor in helping you to pass your test.

EDUCATING AND INTERACTING WITH THE PUBLIC

These questions test for knowledge of techniques used to interact effectively with individual citizens and/or community groups, to educate or inform them about topics of concern, to publicize or clarify agency programs or policies, to negotiate conflicts or resolve complaints, and to represent one's agency or program in a manner in keeping with good public relations practices. Questions may also cover interacting with others in cooperative efforts of public outreach or service. There will be 15 questions in this subject area on the written test.

TEST TASK:
You will be presented with a variety of situations in which you must apply knowledge of how best to interact with other people.

SAMPLE QUESTION:
A person approaches you expressing anger about a recent action by your department. Which one of the following should be your first response to this person?

A. Interrupt to say you cannot discuss the situation until he calms down.
B. Say you are sorry that he has been negatively affected by your department's action.
C. Listen and express understanding that he has been upset by your department's action.
D. Give him an explanation of the reasons for your department's action.

The correct answer to this sample question is choice C

C. SOLUTION:

Choice A *is not correct.* It would be inappropriate to interrupt. In addition, saying that you cannot discuss the situation until the person calms down will likely aggravate him further.

Choice B *is not correct.* Apologizing for your department's action implies that the action was improper.

Choice C is the correct answer to this question. By listening and expressing understanding that your department's action has upset him, you demonstrate that you have heard and understand his feelings and point of view.

Choice D *is not correct.* While an explanation of the reasons for the action may be appropriate at a later time, at this moment the person is angry and would not be receptive to such an explanation.

HOW TO TAKE A TEST

You have studied long, hard and conscientiously.

With your official admission card in hand, and your heart pounding, you have been admitted to the examination room.

You note that there are several hundred other applicants in the examination room waiting to take the same test.

They all appear to be equally well prepared.

You know that nothing but your best effort will suffice. The "moment of truth" is at hand: you now have to demonstrate objectively, in writing, your knowledge of content and your understanding of subject matter.

You are fighting the most important battle of your life—to pass and/or score high on an examination which will determine your career and provide the economic basis for your livelihood.

What extra, special things should you know and should you do in taking the examination?

I. YOU MUST PASS AN EXAMINATION

A. WHAT EVERY CANDIDATE SHOULD KNOW
Examination applicants often ask us for help in preparing for the written test. What can I study in advance? What kinds of questions will be asked? How will the test be given? How will the papers be graded?

B. HOW ARE EXAMS DEVELOPED?
Examinations are carefully written by trained technicians who are specialists in the field known as "psychological measurement," in consultation with recognized authorities in the field of work that the test will cover. These experts recommend the subject matter areas or skills to be tested; only those knowledges or skills important to your success on the job are included. The most reliable books and source materials available are used as references. Together, the experts and technicians judge the difficulty level of the questions.
Test technicians know how to phrase questions so that the problem is clearly stated. Their ethics do not permit "trick" or "catch" questions. Questions may have been tried out on sample groups, or subjected to statistical analysis, to determine their usefulness.
Written tests are often used in combination with performance tests, ratings of training and experience, and oral interviews. All of these measures combine to form the best-known means of finding the right person for the right job.

II. HOW TO PASS THE WRITTEN TEST

A. BASIC STEPS

1) Study the announcement

How, then, can you know what subjects to study? Our best answer is: "Learn as much as possible about the class of positions for which you've applied." The exam will test the knowledge, skills and abilities needed to do the work.

Your most valuable source of information about the position you want is the official exam announcement. This announcement lists the training and experience qualifications. Check these standards and apply only if you come reasonably close to meeting them. Many jurisdictions preview the written test in the exam announcement by including a section called "Knowledge and Abilities Required," "Scope of the Examination," or some similar heading. Here you will find out specifically what fields will be tested.

2) Choose appropriate study materials

If the position for which you are applying is technical or advanced, you will read more advanced, specialized material. If you are already familiar with the basic principles of your field, elementary textbooks would waste your time. Concentrate on advanced textbooks and technical periodicals. Think through the concepts and review difficult problems in your field.

These are all general sources. You can get more ideas on your own initiative, following these leads. For example, training manuals and publications of the government agency which employs workers in your field can be useful, particularly for technical and professional positions. A letter or visit to the government department involved may result in more specific study suggestions, and certainly will provide you with a more definite idea of the exact nature of the position you are seeking.

3) Study this book!

III. KINDS OF TESTS

Tests are used for purposes other than measuring knowledge and ability to perform specified duties. For some positions, it is equally important to test ability to make adjustments to new situations or to profit from training. In others, basic mental abilities not dependent on information are essential. Questions which test these things may not appear as pertinent to the duties of the position as those which test for knowledge and information. Yet they are often highly important parts of a fair examination. For very general questions, it is almost impossible to help you direct your study efforts. What we can do is to point out some of the more common of these general abilities needed in public service positions and describe some typical questions.

1) General information

Broad, general information has been found useful for predicting job success in some kinds of work. This is tested in a variety of ways, from vocabulary lists to questions about current events. Basic background in some field of work, such as sociology or economics, may be sampled in a group of questions. Often these are principles which have become familiar to most persons through exposure rather than through formal training. It is difficult to advise you how to study for these questions; being alert to the world around you is our best suggestion.

2) Verbal ability

An example of an ability needed in many positions is verbal or language ability. Verbal ability is, in brief, the ability to use and understand words. Vocabulary and grammar tests are typical measures of this ability. Reading comprehension or paragraph interpretation questions are common in many kinds of civil service tests. You are given a paragraph of written material and asked to find its central meaning.

IV. KINDS OF QUESTIONS

1. Multiple-choice Questions

Most popular of the short-answer questions is the "multiple choice" or "best answer" question. It can be used, for example, to test for factual knowledge, ability to solve problems or judgment in meeting situations found at work.

A multiple-choice question is normally one of three types:
- It can begin with an incomplete statement followed by several possible endings. You are to find the one ending which best completes the statement, although some of the others may not be entirely wrong.
- It can also be a complete statement in the form of a question which is answered by choosing one of the statements listed.
- It can be in the form of a problem – again you select the best answer.

Here is an example of a multiple-choice question with a discussion which should give you some clues as to the method for choosing the right answer:

When an employee has a complaint about his assignment, the action which will best help him overcome his difficulty is to
- A. discuss his difficulty with his coworkers
- B. take the problem to the head of the organization
- C. take the problem to the person who gave him the assignment
- D. say nothing to anyone about his complaint

In answering this question, you should study each of the choices to find which is best. Consider choice "A" – Certainly an employee may discuss his complaint with fellow employees, but no change or improvement can result, and the complaint remains unresolved. Choice "B" is a poor choice since the head of the organization probably does not know what assignment you have been given, and taking your problem to him is known as "going over the head" of the supervisor. The supervisor, or person who made the assignment, is the person who can clarify it or correct any injustice. Choice "C" is, therefore, correct. To say nothing, as in choice "D," is unwise. Supervisors have and interest in knowing the problems employees are facing, and the employee is seeking a solution to his problem.

2. True/False

3. Matching Questions

Matching an answer from a column of choices within another column.

V. RECORDING YOUR ANSWERS

Computer terminals are used more and more today for many different kinds of exams.

For an examination with very few applicants, you may be told to record your answers in the test booklet itself. Separate answer sheets are much more common. If this separate answer sheet is to be scored by machine – and this is often the case – it is highly important that you mark your answers correctly in order to get credit.

VI. BEFORE THE TEST

YOUR PHYSICAL CONDITION IS IMPORTANT

If you are not well, you can't do your best work on tests. If you are half asleep, you can't do your best either. Here are some tips:

1) Get about the same amount of sleep you usually get. Don't stay up all night before the test, either partying or worrying—DON'T DO IT!
2) If you wear glasses, be sure to wear them when you go to take the test. This goes for hearing aids, too.
3) If you have any physical problems that may keep you from doing your best, be sure to tell the person giving the test. If you are sick or in poor health, you relay cannot do your best on any test. You can always come back and take the test some other time.

Common sense will help you find procedures to follow to get ready for an examination. Too many of us, however, overlook these sensible measures. Indeed, nervousness and fatigue have been found to be the most serious reasons why applicants fail to do their best on civil service tests. Here is a list of reminders:

- Begin your preparation early – Don't wait until the last minute to go scurrying around for books and materials or to find out what the position is all about.
- Prepare continuously – An hour a night for a week is better than an all-night cram session. This has been definitely established. What is more, a night a week for a month will return better dividends than crowding your study into a shorter period of time.
- Locate the place of the exam – You have been sent a notice telling you when and where to report for the examination. If the location is in a different town or otherwise unfamiliar to you, it would be well to inquire the best route and learn something about the building.
- Relax the night before the test – Allow your mind to rest. Do not study at all that night. Plan some mild recreation or diversion; then go to bed early and get a good night's sleep.
- Get up early enough to make a leisurely trip to the place for the test – This way unforeseen events, traffic snarls, unfamiliar buildings, etc. will not upset you.
- Dress comfortably – A written test is not a fashion show. You will be known by number and not by name, so wear something comfortable.
- Leave excess paraphernalia at home – Shopping bags and odd bundles will get in your way. You need bring only the items mentioned in the official notice you received; usually everything you need is provided. Do not bring reference books to the exam. They will only confuse those last minutes and be taken away from you when in the test room.

- Arrive somewhat ahead of time – If because of transportation schedules you must get there very early, bring a newspaper or magazine to take your mind off yourself while waiting.
- Locate the examination room – When you have found the proper room, you will be directed to the seat or part of the room where you will sit. Sometimes you are given a sheet of instructions to read while you are waiting. Do not fill out any forms until you are told to do so; just read them and be prepared.
- Relax and prepare to listen to the instructions
- If you have any physical problem that may keep you from doing your best, be sure to tell the test administrator. If you are sick or in poor health, you really cannot do your best on the exam. You can come back and take the test some other time.

VII. AT THE TEST

The day of the test is here and you have the test booklet in your hand. The temptation to get going is very strong. Caution! There is more to success than knowing the right answers. You must know how to identify your papers and understand variations in the type of short-answer question used in this particular examination. Follow these suggestions for maximum results from your efforts:

1) Cooperate with the monitor

The test administrator has a duty to create a situation in which you can be as much at ease as possible. He will give instructions, tell you when to begin, check to see that you are marking your answer sheet correctly, and so on. He is not there to guard you, although he will see that your competitors do not take unfair advantage. He wants to help you do your best.

2) Listen to all instructions

Don't jump the gun! Wait until you understand all directions. In most civil service tests you get more time than you need to answer the questions. So don't be in a hurry. Read each word of instructions until you clearly understand the meaning. Study the examples, listen to all announcements and follow directions. Ask questions if you do not understand what to do.

3) Identify your papers

Civil service exams are usually identified by number only. You will be assigned a number; you must not put your name on your test papers. Be sure to copy your number correctly. Since more than one exam may be given, copy your exact examination title.

4) Plan your time

Unless you are told that a test is a "speed" or "rate of work" test, speed itself is usually not important. Time enough to answer all the questions will be provided, but this does not mean that you have all day. An overall time limit has been set. Divide the total time (in minutes) by the number of questions to determine the approximate time you have for each question.

5) Do not linger over difficult questions

If you come across a difficult question, mark it with a paper clip (useful to have along) and come back to it when you have been through the booklet. One caution if you do this – be sure to skip a number on your answer sheet as well. Check often to be sure that you have not lost your place and that you are marking in the row numbered the same as the question you are answering.

6) Read the questions
Be sure you know what the question asks! Many capable people are unsuccessful because they failed to read the questions correctly.

7) Answer all questions
Unless you have been instructed that a penalty will be deducted for incorrect answers, it is better to guess than to omit a question.

8) Speed tests
It is often better NOT to guess on speed tests. It has been found that on timed tests people are tempted to spend the last few seconds before time is called in marking answers at random – without even reading them – in the hope of picking up a few extra points. To discourage this practice, the instructions may warn you that your score will be "corrected" for guessing. That is, a penalty will be applied. The incorrect answers will be deducted from the correct ones, or some other penalty formula will be used.

9) Review your answers
If you finish before time is called, go back to the questions you guessed or omitted to give them further thought. Review other answers if you have time.

10) Return your test materials
If you are ready to leave before others have finished or time is called, take ALL your materials to the monitor and leave quietly. Never take any test material with you. The monitor can discover whose papers are not complete, and taking a test booklet may be grounds for disqualification.

VIII. EXAMINATION TECHNIQUES

1) Read the general instructions carefully. These are usually printed on the first page of the exam booklet. As a rule, these instructions refer to the timing of the examination; the fact that you should not start work until the signal and must stop work at a signal, etc. If there are any special instructions, such as a choice of questions to be answered, make sure that you note this instruction carefully.

2) When you are ready to start work on the examination, that is as soon as the signal has been given, read the instructions to each question booklet, underline any key words or phrases, such as least, best, outline, describe and the like. In this way you will tend to answer as requested rather than discover on reviewing your paper that you listed without describing, that you selected the worst choice rather than the best choice, etc.

3) If the examination is of the objective or multiple-choice type – that is, each question will also give a series of possible answers: A, B, C or D, and you are called upon to select the best answer and write the letter next to that answer on your answer paper – it is advisable to start answering each question in turn. There may be anywhere from 50 to 100 such questions in the three or four hours allotted and you can see how much time would be taken if you read through all the questions before beginning to answer any. Furthermore, if you

come across a question or group of questions which you know would be difficult to answer, it would undoubtedly affect your handling of all the other questions.

4) If the examination is of the essay type and contains but a few questions, it is a moot point as to whether you should read all the questions before starting to answer any one. Of course, if you are given a choice – say five out of seven and the like – then it is essential to read all the questions so you can eliminate the two that are most difficult. If, however, you are asked to answer all the questions, there may be danger in trying to answer the easiest one first because you may find that you will spend too much time on it. The best technique is to answer the first question, then proceed to the second, etc.

5) Time your answers. Before the exam begins, write down the time it started, then add the time allowed for the examination and write down the time it must be completed, then divide the time available somewhat as follows:
    - If 3-1/2 hours are allowed, that would be 210 minutes. If you have 80 objective-type questions, that would be an average of 2-1/2 minutes per question. Allow yourself no more than 2 minutes per question, or a total of 160 minutes, which will permit about 50 minutes to review.
    - If for the time allotment of 210 minutes there are 7 essay questions to answer, that would average about 30 minutes a question. Give yourself only 25 minutes per question so that you have about 35 minutes to review.

6) The most important instruction is to read each question and make sure you know what is wanted. The second most important instruction is to time yourself properly so that you answer every question. The third most important instruction is to answer every question. Guess if you have to but include something for each question. Remember that you will receive no credit for a blank and will probably receive some credit if you write something in answer to an essay question. If you guess a letter – say "B" for a multiple-choice question – you may have guessed right. If you leave a blank as an answer to a multiple-choice question, the examiners may respect your feelings but it will not add a point to your score. Some exams may penalize you for wrong answers, so in such cases only, you may not want to guess unless you have some basis for your answer.

7) Suggestions
    a. Objective-type questions
        1. Examine the question booklet for proper sequence of pages and questions
        2. Read all instructions carefully
        3. Skip any question which seems too difficult; return to it after all other questions have been answered
        4. Apportion your time properly; do not spend too much time on any single question or group of questions
        5. Note and underline key words – all, most, fewest, least, best, worst, same, opposite, etc.
        6. Pay particular attention to negatives
        7. Note unusual option, e.g., unduly long, short, complex, different or similar in content to the body of the question
        8. Observe the use of "hedging" words – probably, may, most likely, etc.

9. Make sure that your answer is put next to the same number as the question
10. Do not second-guess unless you have good reason to believe the second answer is definitely more correct
11. Cross out original answer if you decide another answer is more accurate; do not erase until you are ready to hand your paper in
12. Answer all questions; guess unless instructed otherwise
13. Leave time for review

b. Essay questions
1. Read each question carefully
2. Determine exactly what is wanted. Underline key words or phrases.
3. Decide on outline or paragraph answer
4. Include many different points and elements unless asked to develop any one or two points or elements
5. Show impartiality by giving pros and cons unless directed to select one side only
6. Make and write down any assumptions you find necessary to answer the questions
7. Watch your English, grammar, punctuation and choice of words
8. Time your answers; don't crowd material

8) Answering the essay question

Most essay questions can be answered by framing the specific response around several key words or ideas. Here are a few such key words or ideas:

M's: manpower, materials, methods, money, management
P's: purpose, program, policy, plan, procedure, practice, problems, pitfalls, personnel, public relations

a. Six basic steps in handling problems:
1. Preliminary plan and background development
2. Collect information, data and facts
3. Analyze and interpret information, data and facts
4. Analyze and develop solutions as well as make recommendations
5. Prepare report and sell recommendations
6. Install recommendations and follow up effectiveness

b. Pitfalls to avoid
1. Taking things for granted – A statement of the situation does not necessarily imply that each of the elements is necessarily true; for example, a complaint may be invalid and biased so that all that can be taken for granted is that a complaint has been registered
2. Considering only one side of a situation – Wherever possible, indicate several alternatives and then point out the reasons you selected the best one
3. Failing to indicate follow up – Whenever your answer indicates action on your part, make certain that you will take proper follow-up action to see how successful your recommendations, procedures or actions turn out to be
4. Taking too long in answering any single question – Remember to time your answers properly

EXAMINATION SECTION

EDUCATING AND INTERACTING WITH THE PUBLIC

These questions test for knowledge of techniques used to interact effectively with individual citizens and/or community groups, to educate or inform them about topics of concern, to publicize or clarify agency programs or policies, to negotiate conflicts or resolve complaints, and to represent one's agency or program in a manner in keeping with good public relations practices. Questions may also cover interacting with others in cooperative efforts of public outreach or service. There will be 15 questions in this subject area on the written test.

TEST TASK:
You will be presented with a variety of situations in which you must apply knowledge of how best to interact with other people.

SAMPLE QUESTION:
A person approaches you expressing anger about a recent action by your department. Which one of the following should be your first response to this person?

A. Interrupt to say you cannot discuss the situation until he calms down.
B. Say you are sorry that he has been negatively affected by your department's action.
C. Listen and express understanding that he has been upset by your department's action.
D. Give him an explanation of the reasons for your department's action.

The correct answer to this sample question is choice C

C. SOLUTION:

Choice A *is not correct.* It would be inappropriate to interrupt. In addition, saying that you cannot discuss the situation until the person calms down will likely aggravate him further.

Choice B *is not correct.* Apologizing for your department's action implies that the action was improper.

Choice C is the correct answer to this question. By listening and expressing understanding that your department's action has upset him, you demonstrate that you have heard and understand his feelings and point of view.

Choice D *is not correct.* While an explanation of the reasons for the action may be appropriate at a later time, at this moment the person is angry and would not be receptive to such an explanation.

EXAMINATION SECTION
TEST 1

DIRECTIONS: Each question or incomplete statement is followed by several suggested answers or completions. Select the one that BEST answers the question or completes the statement. *PRINT THE LETTER OF THE CORRECT ANSWER IN THE SPACE AT THE RIGHT.*

1. When conducting a needs assessment for the purpose of education planning, an agency's FIRST step is to identify or provide
   A. a profile of population characteristics
   B. barriers to participation
   C. existing resources
   D. profiles of competing resources

   1.____

2. Research has demonstrated that of the following, the MOST effective medium for communicating with external publics is(are)
   A. video news releases
   B. television
   C. radio
   D. newspapers

   2.____

3. Basic ideas behind the effort to influence the attitudes and behaviors of a constituency include each of the following EXCEPT the idea that
   A. words, rather than actions or events, are most likely to motivate
   B. demands for action are a usual response
   C. self-interest usually figures heavily into public involvement
   D. the reliability of change programs is difficult to assess

   3.____

4. An agency representative is trying to craft a pithy message to constituents in order to encourage the use of agency program resources.
   Choosing an audience for such messages is easiest when the message
   A. is project- or behavior-based
   B. is combined with other messages
   C. is abstract
   D. has a broad appeal

   4.____

5. Of the following factors, the MOST important to the success of an agency's external education or communication programs is the
   A. amount of resources used to implement them
   B. public's prior experiences with the agency
   C. real value of the program to the public
   D. commitment of the internal audience

   5.____

6. A representative for a state agency is being interviewed by a reporter from a local news network. The representative is being asked to defend a program that is extremely unpopular in certain parts of the municipality.
   When a constituency is known to be opposed to a position, the MOST useful communication strategy is to present

   6.____

A. only the arguments that are consistent with constituents' views
B. only the agency's side of the issue
C. both sides of the argument as clearly as possible
D. both sides of the argument, omitting key information about the opposing position

7. The MOST significant barriers to effective agency community relations include 7.____
   I. widespread distrust of communication strategies
   II. the media's "watchdog" stance
   III. public apathy
   IV. statutory opposition

   The CORRECT answer is:
   A. I only   B. I and II   C. II and III   D. III and IV

8. In conducting an education program, many agencies use workshops and seminars in a classroom setting. 8.____
   Advantages of classroom-style teaching over other means of educating the public include each of the following, EXCEPT
   A. enabling an instructor to verify learning through testing and interaction with the target audience
   B. enabling hands-on practice and other participatory learning techniques
   C. ability to reach an unlimited number of participants in a given length of time
   D. ability to convey the latest, most up-to-date information

9. The _____ model of community relations is characterized by an attempt to persuade the public to adopt the agency's point of view. 9.____
   A. two-way symmetric   B. two-way asymmetric
   C. public information   D. press agency/publicity

10. Important elements of an internal situation analysis include the 10.____
    I. list of agency opponents   II. communication audit
    III. updated organizational almanac   IV. stakeholder analysis

    The CORRECT answer is:
    A. I and II   B. I, II, and III   C. II and III   D. I, II, III and IV

11. Government agency information efforts typically involve each of the following objectives, EXCEPT to 11.____
    A. implement changes in the policies of government agencies to align with public opinion
    B. communicate the work of agencies
    C. explain agency techniques in a way that invites input from citizens
    D. provide citizen feedback to government administrators

12. Factors that are likely to influence the effectiveness of an educational campaign include the
    I. level of homogeneity among intended participants
    II. number and types of media used
    III. receptivity of the intended participants
    IV. level of specificity in the message or behavior to be taught

    The CORRECT answer is:
    A. I and II   B. I, II, and III   C. II and III   D. I, II, III, and IV

13. An agency representative is writing instructional objectives that will later help to measure the effectiveness of an educational program.
    Which of the following verbs, included in an objective, would be MOST helpful for the purpose of measuring effectiveness?
    A. Know   B. Identify   C. Learn   D. Comprehend

14. A state education agency wants to encourage participation in a program that has just received a boost through new federal legislation. The program is intended to include participants from a wide variety of socioeconomic and other demographic characteristics. The agency wants to launch a broad-based program that will inform virtually every interested party in the state about the program's new circumstances.
    In attempting to deliver this message to such a wide-ranging constituency, the agency's BEST practice would be to
    A. broadcast the same message through as many different media channels as possible
    B. focus on one discrete segment of the public at a time
    C. craft a message whose appeal is as broad as the public itself
    D. let the program's achievements speak for themselves and rely on word-of-mouth

15. Advantages associated with using the World Wide Web as an educational tool include
    I. an appeal to younger generations of the public
    II. visually-oriented, interactive learning
    III. learning that is not confined by space, time, or institutional association
    IV. a variety of methods for verifying use and learning

    The CORRECT answer is:
    A. I only   B. I and II   C. I, II, and III   D. I, II, II, and IV

16. In agencies involved in health care, community relations is a critical function because it
    A. serves as an intermediary between the agency and consumers
    B. generates a clear mission statement for agency goals and priorities
    C. ensures patient privacy while satisfying the media's right to information
    D. helps marketing professionals determine the wants and needs of agency constituents

17. After an extensive campaign to promote its newest program to constituents, an agency learns that most of the audience did not understand the intended message.
MOST likely, the agency has
   A. chosen words that were intended to inform, rather than persuade
   B. not accurately interpreted what the audience really needed to know
   C. overestimated the ability of the audience to receive and process the message
   D. compensated for noise that may have interrupted the message

18. The necessary elements that lead to conviction and motivation in the minds of participants in an educational or information program include each of the following, EXCEPT the _____ of the message.
   A. acceptability   B. intensity
   C. single-channel appeal D. pervasiveness

19. Printed materials are often at the core of educational programs provided by public agencies.
The PRIMARY disadvantage associated with print is that it
   A. does not enable comprehensive treatment of a topic
   B. is generally unreliable in term of assessing results
   C. is often the most expensive medium available
   D. is constrained by time

20. Traditional thinking on public opinion holds that there is about _____ percent of the public who are pivotal to shifting the balance and momentum of opinion—they are concerned about an issue, but not fanatical, and interested enough to pay attention to a reasoned discussion.
   A. 2   B. 10   C. 33   D. 51

21. One of the most useful guidelines for influencing attitude change among people is to
   A. invite the target audience to come to you, rather than approaching them
   B. use moral appeals as the primary approach
   C. use concrete images to enable people to see the results of behaviors or indifference
   D. offer tangible rewards to people for changes in behavior

22. An agency is attempting to evaluate the effectiveness of its educational program. For this purpose, it wants to observe several focus groups discussing the same program.
Which of the following would NOT be a guideline for the use of focus groups?
   A. Focus groups should only include those who have participated in the program.
   B. Be sure to accurately record the discussion.
   C. The same questions should be asked at each focus group meeting.
   D. It is often helpful to have a neutral, non-agency employee facilitate discussions.

23. Research consistently shows that _____ is the determinant most likely to make a newspaper editor run a news release.
    A. novelty   B. prominence   C. proximity   D. conflict

24. Which of the following is NOT one of the major variables to take into account when considering a population-needs assessment?
    A. State of program development   B. Resources available
    C. Demographics   D. Community attitudes

25. The FIRST step in any communications audit is to
    A. develop a research instrument
    B. determine how the organization currently communicates
    C. hire a contractor
    D. determine which audience to assess

KEY (CORRECT ANSWERS)

1. A
2. D
3. A
4. A
5. D

6. C
7. D
8. C
9. B
10. C

11. A
12. D
13. B
14. B
15. C

16. A
17. B
18. C
19. B
20. B

21. C
22. A
23. C
24. C
25. D

TEST 2

DIRECTIONS: Each question or incomplete statement is followed by several suggested answers or completions. Select the one that BEST answers the question or completes the statement. *PRINT THE LETTER OF THE CORRECT ANSWER IN THE SPACE AT THE RIGHT.*

1. A public relations practitioner at an agency has just composed a press release highlighting a program's recent accomplishments and success stories.
   In pitching such releases to print outlets, the practitioner should
   I. e-mail, mail, or send them by messenger
   II. address them to "editor" or "news director"
   III. have an assistant call all media contacts by telephone
   IV. ask reporters or editors how they prefer to receive them

   The CORRECT answer is:
   A. I and II   B. I and IV   C. II, III, and IV   D. III only

   1.____

2. The "output goals" of an educational program are MOST likely to include
   A. specified ratings of services by participants on a standardized scale
   B. observable effects on a given community or clientele
   C. the number of instructional hours provided
   D. the number of participants served

   2.____

3. An agency wants to evaluate satisfaction levels among program participants, and mails out questionnaires to everyone who has been enrolled in the last year.
   The PRIMARY problem associated with this method of evaluative research is that it
   A. poses a significant inconvenience for respondents
   B. is inordinately expensive
   C. does not allow for follow-up or clarification questions
   D. usually involves a low response rate

   3.____

4. A communications audit is an important tool for measuring
   A. the depth of penetration of a particular message or program
   B. the cost of the organization's information campaigns
   C. how key audiences perceive an organization
   D. the commitment of internal stakeholders

   4.____

5. The "ABCs" of written learning objectives include each of the following, EXCEPT
   A. Audience   B. Behavior   C. Conditions   D. Delineation

   5.____

6. When attempting to change the behaviors of constituents, it is important to keep in mind that
    I. most people are skeptical of communications that try to get them to change their behaviors
    II. in most cases, a person selects the media to which he exposes himself
    III. people tend to react defensively to messages or programs that rely on fear as a motivating factor
    IV. programs should aim for the broadest appeal possible in order to include as many participants as possible

    The CORRECT answer is:
    A. I and II   B. I, II and III   C. II and III   D. I, II, III, and IV

7. The "laws" of public opinion include the idea that it is
    A. useful for anticipating emergencies
    B. not sensitive to important events
    C. basically determined by self-interest
    D. sustainable through persistent appeals

8. Which of the following types of evaluations is used to measure public attitudes before and after an information/educational program?
    A. Retrieval study
    B. Copy test
    C. Quota sampling
    D. Benchmark study

9. The PRIMARY source for internal communications is(are) usually
    A. flow charts
    B. meetings
    C. voice mail
    D. printed publications

10. An agency representative is putting together informational materials—brochures and a newsletter—outlining changes in one of the state's biggest benefits programs.
    In assembling print materials as a medium for delivering information to the public, the representative should keep in mind each of the following trends:
    I. For various reasons, the reading capabilities of the public are in general decline
    II. Without tables and graphs to help illustrate the changes, it is unlikely that the message will be delivered effectively
    III. Professionals and career-oriented people are highly receptive to information written in the form of a journal article or empirical study
    IV. People tend to be put off by print materials that use itemized and bulleted (●) lists

    The CORRECT answer is:
    A. I and II   B. I, II and III   C. II and III   D. I, II, III, and IV

11. Which of the following steps in a problem-oriented information campaign would typically be implemented FIRST?
    A. Deciding on tactics
    B. Determining a communications strategy
    C. Evaluating the problem's impact
    D. Developing an organizational strategy

12. A common pitfall in conducting an educational program is to
    A. aim it at the wrong target audience
    B. overfund it
    C. leave it in the hands of people who are in the business of education, rather than those with expertise in the business of the organization
    D. ignore the possibility that some other organization is meeting the same educational need for the target audience

13. The key factors that affect the credibility of an agency's educational program include
    A. organization
    B. scope
    C. sophistication
    D. penetration

14. Research on public opinion consistently demonstrates that it is
    A. easy to move people toward a strong opinion on anything, as long as they are approached directly through their emotions
    B. easier to move people away from an opinion they currently hold than to have them form an opinion about something they have not previously cared about
    C. easy to move people toward a strong opinion on anything, as long as the message appeals to their reason and intellect
    D. difficult to move people toward a strong opinion on anything, no matter what the approach

15. In conducting an education program, many agencies use meetings and conferences to educate an audience about the organization and its programs. Advantages associated with this approach include
    I. a captive audience that is known to be interested in the topic
    II. ample opportunities for verifying learning
    III. cost-efficient meeting space
    IV. the ability to provide information on a wider variety of subjects

    The CORRECT answer is:
    A. I and II   B. I, III and IV   C. II and III   D. I, II, III and IV

16. An agency is attempting to evaluate the effectiveness of its educational programs. For this purpose, it wants to observe several focus groups discussing particular programs.
    For this purpose, a focus group should never number more than _____ participants.
    A. 5   B. 10   C. 15   D. 20

17. A _____ speech is written so that several agency members can deliver it to different audiences with only minor variations.
    A. basic   B. printed   C. quota   D. pattern

18. Which of the following statements about public opinion is generally considered to be FALSE?
    A. Opinion is primarily reactive rather than proactive.
    B. People have more opinions about goals than about the means by which to achieve them.
    C. Facts tend to shift opinion in the accepted direction when opinion is not solidly structured.
    D. Public opinion is based more on information than desire.

19. An agency is trying to promote its educational program.
    As a general rule, the agency should NOT assume that
    A. people will only participate if they perceive an individual benefit
    B. promotions need to be aimed at small, discrete groups
    C. if the program is good, the audience will find out about it
    D. a variety of methods, including advertising, special events, and direct mail, should be considered

20. In planning a successful educational program, probably the first and most important question for an agency to ask is:
    A. What will be the content of the program?
    B. Who will be served by the program?
    C. When is the best time to schedule the program?
    D. Why is the program necessary?

21. Media kits are LEAST likely to contain
    A. fact sheets   B. memoranda
    C. photographs with captions   D. news releases

22. The use of pamphlets and booklets as media for communication with the public often involves the disadvantage that
    A. the messages contained within them are frequently nonspecific
    B. it is difficult to measure their effectiveness in delivering the message
    C. there are few opportunities for people to refer to them
    D. color reproduction is poor

23. The MOST important prerequisite of a good educational program is an
    A. abundance of resources to implement it
    B. individual staff unit formed for the purpose of program delivery
    C. accurate needs assessment
    D. uneducated constituency

24. After an education program has been delivered, an agency conducts a program evaluation to determine whether its objectives have been met.
General rules about how to conduct such an education program valuation include each of the following, EXCEPT that it
   A. must be done immediately after the program has been implemented
   B. should be simple and easy to use
   C. should be designed so that tabulation of responses can take place quickly and inexpensively
   D. should solicit mostly subjective, open-ended responses if the audience was large

24.____

25. Using electronic media such as television as means of educating the public is typically recommended ONLY for agencies that
   I. have a fairly simple message to begin with
   II. want to reach the masses, rather than a targeted audience
   III. have substantial financial resources
   IV. accept that they will not be able to measure the results of the campaign with much precision

   The CORRECT answer is:
   A. I and II   B. I, II and III   C. II and IV   D. I, II, III and IV

25.____

KEY (CORRECT ANSWERS)

1.	B		11.	C
2.	C		12.	D
3.	D		13.	A
4.	C		14.	D
5.	D		15.	B
6.	B		16.	B
7.	C		17.	D
8.	D		18.	D
9.	D		19.	C
10.	A		20.	D

21.	B
22.	B
23.	C
24.	D
25.	D

EXAMINATION SECTION
TEST 1

DIRECTIONS: Each question or incomplete statement is followed by several suggested answers or completions. Select the one that BEST answers the question or completes the statement. *PRINT THE LETTER OF THE CORRECT ANSWER IN THE SPACE AT THE RIGHT.*

1. Which of the following is a behavior that can impact customer service? 1.____
   A. Greeting customers promptly
   B. Believing in a positive mission statement
   C. Giving great service
   D. Poor work attitude

2. What are vital behaviors? 2.____
   A. Ones that are mandated by law
   B. Specific actions that have the maximum impact on customer service
   C. Of no particular importance when influencing employees
   D. The same as good attitudes

3. Of the following, the MOST effective icebreaker when greeting a local citizen in your office would be: 3.____
   A. Talking about local interests such as a sports team or the weather
   B. Expression appreciation for the citizen visiting you today
   C. Finding out and expressing interest in something the citizen shows interest in
   D. All of the above

4. Which of the following actions would get citizens to interact with you and, therefore, the government you represent? 4.____
   A. Inviting the citizens to fill out a survey on government services
   B. Helping the citizen find answers to questions about your department
   C. Both A and B
   D. None of the above

5. Of the following options, the BIGGEST issue with not greeting a citizen promptly is: 5.____
   A. He or she might not leave as quickly as you'd like them to
   B. The department misses an opportunity to establish a positive relationship
   C. They may estimate that their wait was shorter than it actually was
   D. Both A and C

6. Which of the following actions is important to take when someone makes an oral presentation to a large group of local residents? 6.____
   A. Relax the audience by moving back and forth when speaking
   B. Avoid eye contact with anyone in the audience
   C. Speak loudly enough for all to hear your message
   D. Turn your back to the audience when presenting visual aids

7. Of the following techniques for writing effective communication (i.e., letters about local tax bills) to residents, which of the following helps a person consistently stay on message the MOST?
   A. Preparing outlines
   B. Development and inclusion of charts
   C. Consulting references
   D. Asking questions

   7.____

8. Persuasive messages that ask a person to do something should be communicated in a way that makes it easy for that person to
   A. plan accordingly
   B. answer politely
   C. organize logically
   D. respond positively

   8.____

9. If a city department wishes to emphasize customer service skills such as courtesy and friendliness, when should said department focus on these skills?
   A. When designing their facilities
   B. During market research
   C. When meeting for technology planning
   D. During the hiring process

   9.____

10. If a department realizes it needs to improve its technology to better meet resident demands and desires, this would have to result from a business activity known as
    A. continuity improvement
    B. business process management
    C. employee training and in-service
    D. organizational positioning

    10.____

11. When in the distribution channel business, what is an important thing to keep in mind concerning customers?
    A. Most expect low service levels
    B. Many want immediate delivery
    C. Everyone defines service differently
    D. A number of customers tend to refuse late shipments

    11.____

12. When persuading a citizen to go along with a proposed change from their initial query, you should
    A. explain how the change will benefit them
    B. tell them you have a better way of doing things
    C. minimize the amount of information you share with them
    D. reinforce your ideas with facts and statistics

    12.____

13. Which of the following statements is TRUE regarding use of the internet to administer questionnaires?
    A. Interviewers are more likely to influence respondents' answers online
    B. Online questionnaires require more time for data entry and collection
    C. Respondents are more likely to misunderstand online questionnaires
    D. Data entry and administrative costs are higher for online questionnaires

    13.____

14. After a series of notable scandals, a government organization wants the public to perceive it as more trustworthy and embarks on an advertising campaign to aid the makeover. What goal does this illustrate?
    A. Projecting a certain image
    B. Achieving stability
    C. Increasing customer service and productivity
    D. All of the above

14._____

15. When presenting information to a small group of town residents, you decide to use presentation software to prepare your multimedia presentation.
    What is the purpose of using this software?
    A. To develop websites
    B. To maintain customer files
    C. To access online resources
    D. To support your report findings

15._____

16. A current trend in interaction with citizens in order to build loyal customer relationships and enhance service levels focuses on optimizing the use of
    A. independent agents
    B. internet web sites
    C. satellite roving devices
    D. service rating advisors

16._____

17. Which of the following would be an excellent example of a parks department official empathizing with a citizen's objection?
    A. "I understand how you feel."
    B. "You must think the price is too high."
    C. "Everyone knows this is how this process works."
    D. "I really don't see what you don't understand about this."

17._____

18. Customer service experts who use the services and products they are in charge of dispensing are able to suggest appropriate substitute services and products because of their own personal
    A. preference
    B. feelings
    C. experience
    D. opinion

18._____

19. An official should always attempt to answer a citizen's questions thoroughly and explain the benefits of their services so that the citizen will
    A. make a quicker decision
    B. be in a state of indecision
    C. think about making a decision
    D. feel better about the decision

19._____

20. One should be able to adjust his customer-service style from one citizen to another so that he can appeal to each citizen's
    A. natural aptitude
    B. unique personality
    C. hidden objection
    D. internal ability

20._____

21. In order to attract local residents and encourage them to make use of a new recreation facility, what should a parks department director do?
    A. Market the site's benefits
    B. Host trade shows
    C. Distribute press kits
    D. Host special community events

21._____

22. What kind of question is a person asking if they ask the following: "What level of service would you like today?" 22._____
    A. Interpretive	B. Impersonal
    C. Open-ended	D. Assumptive

23. Your department holds a meeting to identify community issues with which they can involve themselves. 23._____
    Which of the following options should the department consider when deciding which community issue to involve themselves with?
    It should
    A. contribute to the social good	B. earn a reasonable profit
    C. boost loyalty among citizens	D. support controversial topics

24. If a person's thoughts, emotions and physical sensations interfere with their listening skills, that is referred to as 24._____
    A. cultural diversity	B. internal noise
    C. cultural norms	D. external noise

25. Which of the following is NOT a characteristic of information literacy? 25._____
    The ability to
    A. use information to manipulate others
    B. determine what information is needed for a presentation
    C. find information relevant to a topic
    D. use information to create new knowledge

KEY (CORRECT ANSWERS)

1. A
2. B
3. D
4. C
5. B

6. C
7. A
8. D
9. D
10. B

11. C
12. A
13. C
14. A
15. D

16. B
17. A
18. C
19. D
20. B

21. D
22. C
23. A
24. B
25. A

TEST 2

DIRECTIONS: Each question or incomplete statement is followed by several suggested answers or completions. Select the one that BEST answers the question or completes the statement. *PRINT THE LETTER OF THE CORRECT ANSWER IN THE SPACE AT THE RIGHT.*

1. When preparing to deliver a speech, what is the purpose of writing key points on notecards and then placing those cards in order of their importance? 1.____
    A. To verify their authenticity
    B. To access files
    C. To revise facts
    D. To organize information

2. A city official who is originally from Ecuador meets with a citizen who has moved to the area from London, England. When the official attempts to shake the citizen's hand, he backs away. 2.____
   What cultural issue should the official be aware of next time to avoid this misstep?
    A. Punctuality
    B. Personal space preferences
    C. Appearance
    D. Language variances

3. Someone who demonstrates self-confidence has which of the following characteristics? 3.____
    A. They take few risks because they fear making mistakes
    B. They exhibit aggressive behavior when expressing their opinion
    C. They realize that mistakes are a part of personal growth
    D. They are overly concerned with what others say about them

4. A town clerk is talking with a resident about fees associated with filing a building permit when the resident interrupts and says, "I refuse to pay for this. These fees are preposterous!" 4.____
   If the clerk wishes to reply in the most professional manner possible, they should do which of the following?
    A. Attempt to explain the benefits of the service
    B. Stop helping the resident and find someone else to help
    C. Ask a supervisor to help convince the resident of the service's merits
    D. Thank the resident politely for coming in

5. You are working with a village resident who asks you questions about aspects of zoning ordinances that you are clearly not familiar with. A coworker overhears the conversation and offers to help. 5.____
   What is the FIRST thing you should do?
    A. Politely refuse the help and attempt to answer the resident's questions anyway
    B. Accept the offer of help and listen to the answers the coworker gives to the resident
    C. Ignore the coworker; they only want to look good in front of your supervisor
    D. Let the other associate take over and look for a new resident to help

6. A resident comes up to an employee in the public works department holding his village-issued recycling container. He says he received the pail a month ago and it already has a cracked handle. As a result his lawn is constantly littered with plastic bottles.
   What is the FIRST thing the employee should say?
   A. "There's no reason it should be cracked. We should have another; I will check for you."
   B. "We've never had anyone make this complaint before. What did you or your child do to it?"
   C. "Are you sure you the village provided this pail? Do you have a receipt?"
   D. "We've had a lot of issues with that item. You should probably contact the manufacturer."

6._____

7. When a person first encounters an employee and forms a lasting mental image of that employee and, therefore, the organization, that is called
   A. attitude impact   B. self-confidence
   C. first impression   D. workplace ethics

7._____

8. Which of the following convey to citizens that their representative is professional?
   A. No wrinkles, creases or stains   B. No large, loud prints
   C. Well-tailored, formal clothing   D. All of the above

8._____

9. A town clerk is put in charge of email communications for the department and asks you for help.
   Which of the following would NOT be considered good email etiquette?
   A. Keeping emails brief and to the point
   B. Putting the purpose of the email in the subject field
   C. Sending humorous YouTube videos and personal emails to customers
   D. Using a signature that includes contact information that follows your message

9._____

10. A building department director is holding a meeting for individual building managers and is just about to conclude when another manager shows up late.
    Which of the following actions would be the BEST to take?
    A. Thank the manager for stopping by and pause the meeting momentarily to fill him or her in on what they missed.
    B. Once the meeting is over, remind the manager that punctuality is incredibly important to your department. Then once they seem to understand the importance of being on time, fill them in on what they missed.
    C. Openly criticize the manager in front of everyone else for being tardy. Once you've criticized them, fill them in on what they missed.
    D. Slightly nod to the manager when they enter, but continue the meeting without bringing them up to speed. Once the meeting concludes, fill the manager in if the wish to be brought up to speed.

10._____

11. You are running 15 minutes late to a meeting with a constituent.   11._____
    What should you do?
    A. Call the constituent and tell them you will be there in a few minutes.
    B. The constituent won't mind waiting. Fifteen minutes is not that long of a wait.
    C. Have your coworker talk to the constituent and tell them you were involved in a minor traffic accident that is causing you to be delayed.
    D. Pretend like you thought the meeting was supposed to be on a different day. Send an email apologizing for the inconvenience.

12. A longtime friend has stopped at your work to visit you before they fly home.   12._____
    You are currently meeting with the local civic association when he shows up.
    What should you do?
    A. Have your friend join the meeting and introduce him to the group.
    B. Tell your friend to wait in the break room/cafeteria and meet him when you finish up your meeting.
    C. Stop the meeting immediately and tell the group to reschedule with you tomorrow. You also let them know they will have priority in terms of meeting times.
    D. Speed through the rest of the meeting and do not stop to ask if anyone has any questions. Then find your friend afterwards.

13. A fellow clerk is filling out forms with a local resident when you notice your favorite   13._____
    song starts playing from your computer. You
    A. dance around the office after blasting the music on your speakers
    B. listen to the music with your headphones at a loud volume so that the clerk and resident can hear a muted version of the song
    C. listen to the music with your headphones in at a low volume so that you do not disturb others and are still accessible in case you are needed
    D. listen to your music with noise-cancelling headphones, so that you cannot hear others if they request your attention

14. As recreation director, you have an important meeting with members of a local   14._____
    youth sports organization and all agree to meet around dinner time.
    Where should you bring them for the dinner meeting?
    A. Ask them their preference for food and pick the corresponding restaurant
    B. An upscale French restaurant known for its romantic ambience
    C. A sports bar that will be airing an important playoff game
    D. Order Chinese food and invite them to the office

15. A city employee has an important presentation in front of a community group today, but   15._____
    it is also "Casual Friday."
    How should the employee dress? Why?
    A. Dress casually. The residents will understand that Casual Fridays are for casual dress, so they will not be upset.
    B. Business casual. A city employee wants to assure the community that they handle business the way they dress, which means a smart, but comfortable look.

C. A little nicer than normally, but nothing too formal. This way they are still comfortable, but the residents know that they are important too.
D. Dress in pajamas. The group does not care what an employee wears as long as their presentation is good.

16. Professionally, what is the longest it should take someone to respond to a resident's email? How about a phone call?
    A. 45 minutes; 15 minutes
    B. 24 hours; 24 hours
    C. 48 hours; 24 hours
    D. 24 hours; 4 hours

16.____

17. Unlike social etiquette, office and business professionalism are PRIMARILY based on
    A. hierarchy and power
    B. personal relations between employees and customers
    C. common sense and courtesy
    D. both A and C

17.____

18. If something goes wrong during interaction with or presentation for a local community group, what should you do?
    A. Clear your head, focus, and be cheerful and professional and act like nothing went wrong
    B. Take responsibility and take appropriate action
    C. Blame others for your technical difficulties
    D. Find a way to end the interaction as quickly as possible

18.____

19. What is the ultimate goal of customer service?
    A. Customer satisfaction
    B. Understanding customers
    C. Identify problems
    D. Improve product and service

19.____

20. Of the following, which is the BEST reason for office employees and supervisors to frequently gauge customer satisfaction?
    A. No reason. One evaluation is enough.
    B. Because employees are not always honest about reporting customer satisfaction.
    C. They may have concerns or complaints that they have not voiced.
    D. Complaints do not always reach management.

20.____

21. Which of the following is TRUE of scope of influence?
    A. It is objective.
    B. Some have a larger scope of influence than others.
    C. Everyone has the same scope of influence.
    D. It is not relevant to customer service.

21.____

22. Which of the following techniques will create credibility in the minds of local residents in regards to their government representatives?
    A. Never admit being wrong. It undermines credibility.
    B. Demonstrate your human emotions. Whether you're angry or happy, let others see it.

22.____

C. Tell people what they want to hear even if it is not necessarily what you know to be true.
D. Become an expert about various factors in your profession. People will respect your knowledge.

23. You are in a "train the trainer" meeting about meeting customer expectations. As you talk in small groups after a short presentation, four people express very different statements about customer expectations.
Which one is CORRECT?
   A. "Wrong. Customer expectations are always changing."
   B. "Customer expectations rarely change."
   C. "Guys, all you really have to do is make a promise to solve customer problems. They forget after a while, even if you don't follow through."
   D. "Do not worry about what other companies are doing. We should focus on ourselves."

23._____

24. Of the following, which of the following is TRUE concerning customer service?
   A. Average customer service will always suffice.
   B. Customers lost through poor customer service are easy to replace.
   C. Organizations must provide excellent customer service or expect failure.
   D. None of the above

24._____

25. You are in a tense conversation with a very upset and aggressive resident. How should you handle this situation?
   A. Make them respect and value your time.
   B. Avoid admitting any wrongdoing on your part.
   C. Find a solution and implement it.
   D. Do not show empathy.

25._____

KEY (CORRECT ANSWERS)

1.	D	11.	A
2.	B	12.	B
3.	C	13.	C
4.	A	14.	A
5.	B	15.	B
6.	A	16.	D
7.	C	17.	D
8.	D	18.	B
9.	C	19.	A
10.	D	20.	C

21. B
22. D
23. A
24. C
25. C

EXAMINATION SECTION

TEST 1

DIRECTIONS: Each question or incomplete statement is followed by several suggested answers or completions. Select the one that BEST answers the question or completes the statement. *PRINT THE LETTER OF THE CORRECT ANSWER IN THE SPACE AT THE RIGHT.*

1. A DMV clerk is assisting a customer who is seeking to renew his driver's license. The customer becomes agitated and confrontational over how long it is taking. Which of the following would be the BEST response for a positive outcome in this situation?
   A. Tell the customer to leave and come back when he is in a better mood
   B. Attempt to de-escalate the situation while also efficiently completing the renewal
   C. Explain that policy does not allow the workers to move any faster
   D. See if another employee can take over while avoiding direct contact with the hostile customer

   1._____

2. A village employee fields a call and question about an upcoming event at Town Hall for which he does not know the answer.
   Which is the BEST response for him to make?
   A. "Great question; let me find that out for you right now!"
   B. "Oh that is a good question...I don't know."
   C. "You need to call back later when a supervisor can answer your question."
   D. "What a good question! Unfortunately, I'm new here and don't know all of the policies. If you call back in a few days I should be able to help."

   2._____

3. A customer walks into the post office and wants to buy the new limited-edition collectible stamps, but they were not shipped on time so the postal clerk will not have them for another few days.
   What should the clerk do to remedy this situation?
   A. Tell the customer the stamps are back-ordered and that he cannot provide any further assistance on the matter
   B. Apologize and offer to give the customer a list of phone numbers for regional post offices to see if they have the stamps
   C. Apologize for the delay and give the customer the specific date that the stamps will be available
   D. Tell the customer the post office operates on a first-come, first-serve basis and she'll have to check back each day if she wants to make sure they received the stamps

   3._____

4. A translator for the Department of Justice receives a call from someone seeking information about one of his family members, but is unable to fully meet the needs of the caller because of the translator's unfamiliarity with the speaker's dialect.

   4._____

How should the translator handle this situation?
- A. "Sir, I am sorry but I'm going to have to transfer you to someone else."
- B. "Hi, sorry to interrupt, but you will need to call back with someone who can speak a little more clearly."
- C. "Hello, just to be clear, I am having a lot of trouble understanding you. Would you mind if I transfer you to someone else?"
- D. "Hello, Mr. [Last Name]! Let's get this problem resolved for you. I'm going to transfer you to a senior linguist that specializes in your specific dialect. They will be able to best aid you."

5. A doctor for the Department of Veterans Affairs is working with a patient who asks her to prescribe some extra medication to help with his pain. The doctor has already given him the appropriate amount.
   What should the doctor do?
   - A. Explain that as much as she'd like to fulfill the patient's request, the medication policy in place is too important as it deals with the patient's safety and health
   - B. Ignore the request and pretend as though she didn't hear the patient
   - C. Give the patient the medication if he obviously needs it for pain management
   - D. Report the patient to the police and have him arrested for attempting to possess controlled substances

5.____

6. A local resident comes into Village Hall upset because someone issued him the wrong permit for a deck renovation on his house.
   As someone who did NOT issue the permit, how should the employee handle this situation?
   - A. Ask the resident to show proof of the wrong permit and then ask what permit he should have
   - B. Explain to the resident that it could not have been the fault of the Village Hall employee and that he [the resident] must have submitted the wrong application
   - C. Tell the resident how sorry he is that this happened, attempt to explain what could have happened and then resolve the situation by approving the correct permit
   - D. Find out who issued the wrong permit and explain that the employee was wrong, then find the employee and have them fix their mistake

6.____

7. A local park district that recently joined Twitter has received public backlash from its residents due to poor communication. In one specific instance, a children's art class was canceled, but the park district did not announce it until after the event would have started and did not offer refunds.
   How should the person in charge of the Twitter account respond to angry residents who have complained about the lack of communication?
   - A. Tell them to contact the park district anytime between 9 A.M. and 5 P.M., which are the normal operating hours
   - B. Post a silly meme that makes fun of the park district's slow response and also acts as an apology

7.____

C. Put out a message that apologizes for tardiness, assures better communication and offers a discount on future programs
D. Tweet out an offer of a partial refund (for the missed class), a sincere apology and a promise to communicate better going forward

8. A postal employee overhears a customer at the post office make the following statement to a co-worker who has Chinese ancestry: "Are you Shu? Or Mou? I can never tell you guys apart!" The customer seems jovial and not angry, but it is clear the co-worker is bothered by this interaction.
What should the employee do?
    A. Yell at the customer and tell him to come back when he is not so racist
    B. Take over for the co-worker and explain to the customer that she would be glad to help, but only on the basis of mutual respect
    C. Attempt to explain to the customer that his joke is prejudiced and unacceptable
    D. Ignore the situation and try to comfort the co-worker after the customer has left

8.____

9. A female Village Hall clerk has been working with a resident all day and has built up a rapport with him while assisting with his issue. As their business starts to conclude, the resident asks if the clerk would like to grab a bite to eat or some coffee after they're done for the day. The clerk is uncomfortable and unsure of what to do.
How should she respond?
    A. "Oh, I'm so tired and I think someone else can handle the rest of your business today."
    B. "That is thoughtful of you, but I'd like to keep this professional and focus on finishing up our business here."
    C. "I suppose we could grab a small bite to eat before I head home."
    D. "Please do not ask me out on a date! You are completely out of line!"

9.____

10. A participant in one of the town-run youth leagues broke his arm two days before the league was set to kick off. Because of the injury, he will be unable to participate, so the boy's mother asks the youth league director for a refund. The mother signed a waiver that clearly states that no refunds can be issued for the league within a week of it starting. Despite this, she asks for an exception because of the circumstance.
What should the league director do?
    A. Attempt to explain why the policy is the way it is, show he understands the frustration of the parent, but reiterate that nothing can be done
    B. Empathize with the parent and show agreement with her, but explain that is not something that can be changed by one person and promise to take this to a superior to solve the issue
    C. Make it clear that an alternative to the policy will be sought, offer another league or activity that the boy could be a part of, or waive the cost of the league for the next year
    D. Explain that the boy and parent should have been more aware of activities that might cause injury and share educational materials on injury prevention and rehabilitation

10.____

11. An employee that works for the state's tourism department receives a phone call from a potential tourist asking for information about attractions. As he starts to answer, the caller interrupts, asks inappropriate questions, and seems to be trying to frustrate the employee.
How should this situation be handled?
    A. He should play it cool by explaining that they would love to answer any actual questions if the caller is being sincere, and if insincere, explain that he needs to attend to other callers who have legitimate questions
    B. He should stay civil and answer all questions the caller has
    C. He should become aggressive and rude back to the caller before hanging up
    D. He should tell the caller he will be right back, but leave the caller on hold indefinitely

11.____

12. An employee in the Citizen Service and Response Department for a town in Virginia handles non-emergency citizen service requests. Recently, the employee received praise via Twitter for an expedient solution to a child's need, but the employee was not the one who actually solved the citizen's problem.
What should she do?
    A. Denounce the tweet as false and tweet about the person who deserves the praise
    B. Take credit for the tweet, but be sure to mention others that were involved
    C. Reach out to the citizen outside of social media and explain who the real hero was
    D. Express gratitude for the recognition, but highlight the coworker who was truly responsible

12.____

13. A resident complains to you that your facility is making exaggerated and false claims about the benefits of joining their exercise classes. She wants you to immediately take down the advertisement and publicly apologize for misleading the community.
What should you do?
    A. Refer her to your supervisor – this is well above your pay grade
    B. Act like you are interested, but dismiss the resident's claim as crazy and does not warrant taking action
    C. Listen with an open mind and determine if there is any truth to the resident's claims. Make a promise to look into the matter, but do not commit to changing anything.
    D. Immediately take down the advertisement and issue the apology. Residents' tax dollars are responsible for the funding you receive, so you cannot risk angering them.

13.____

14. A customer becomes confused as to which line he is supposed to be on at the DMV. After a lengthy wait, the man arrives at your station for a driver's license renewal, but you explain you are working on license-plate services only. He slumps his shoulders and displays some distress before imploring you to make an exception for him so he does not have to go back to the end of the line and start all over.
    What should you do?
    A. Tell him you would love to help, but going against policy could negatively impact your performance review
    B. Garner the attention of your co-worker who is working license renewals and have him put the customer higher up in his queue
    C. Repeat your initial statement that he is in the wrong line, then ignore his request and ask for the next customer in line
    D. Leave your post and have the customer follow. Explain the situation to your co-worker working at license renewal and have the customer jump to the front of the line.

    14.____

15. A Village Hall employee is talking on the phone with a resident who needs help registering for a program electronically, but during the discussion the employee realizes the resident is not at home and does not have access to necessary registration information.
    How should the employee proceed?
    A. Direct the customer to look for the answer on the village's website when she is at home
    B. Hang up on the caller – obviously, she does not know what she is doing and does not deserve the help
    C. Tell the customer that she cannot be helped until she has the correct information, then end the call
    D. Establish a time for the person to call back when she is able to provide the relevant information

    15.____

16. An employee at the Recreational Center receives a phone call from a resident who says, "I am very upset that my meeting with your service director did not start at the appointed time. I was told the meeting would start at 11:30 A.M. and he did not arrive until 12:15 P.M. I took the morning off from work to make this meeting, but I did not need to if I had known the meeting was going to be so late!" After politely putting the person on hold, the employee calls the director who tells her the meeting began late because of heavy traffic and a previous meeting that had run long.
    Once the employee takes the resident off hold, how should she respond?
    A. Offer sincere apologies and explain what happened without making excuses for the late start to the meeting
    B. Apologize profusely to the resident, but give the contact information for the director, so the director can explain what happened
    C. Tell the resident that sometimes meetings run late and that she could have left if she wanted to, as it was a voluntary meeting
    D. Ask the resident what she would like the employee to do about the situation

    16.____

17. An elderly customer calls the post office with a problem finding some product information on the website. He is polite yet frustrated and upset that he cannot find the information he is seeking. The post office employee recognizes what the elderly man is looking for, but realizes the information is too long and complicated to share over the phone.
What are the BEST steps for the employee to take?
    A. Tell him he can find the information he is looking for in the product information section of the website
    B. Offer to find the specific information he needs and e-mail it to him directly
    C. Advise him to go to the product information section of the website and print out all of the available material so that he can review it offline
    D. Send him a link to a video tutorial that shows customers how to navigate the post office website

17.____

18. A DMV clerk is attempting to explain procedures to a customer that seems to be hard of hearing. The clerk explains twice, but the customer does not seem to understand.
What should the clerk do?
    A. Explain that he is not sure what the customer does not understand and walk away
    B. Ask someone else to help the customer
    C. Repeat the procedures for the third time and try to explain it slightly differently or with written instructions
    D. Repeat the procedures for the third time and then ask for the next customer in line

18.____

19. A resident is considering signing up for a fitness program through the park district, though the trainer running the program knows it will not completely fulfill the customer's needs.
What should the trainer do?
    A. Alert the resident to what the program will actually cover and explain that it is still worth the customer's time even if it doesn't fully meet what he is looking for
    B. Answer any questions the customer may have, but do nothing else, as the trainer can support the customer after they've started
    C. Suggest that a non-district fitness program might be better and offer to find the information for him
    D. Make any promises and guarantees about the program that is needed. Once he signs up, the customer is not the employee's concern anymore.

19.____

20. A resident comes into a county clerk's office looking upset and distraught. How can the clerk display active listening skills so the resident can at least know that her voice was heard?
    A. Nod and make eye contact as the resident tells her story
    B. Frequently ask the resident if she would like any water or snacks while she tells her story
    C. Use phrases like "I see" or "Go on" whenever it seems to be an appropriate pause
    D. Both A and C

20.____

21. A public defense attorney meets with a client who becomes aggressive and combative when the attorney asks for clarification on an event that the client was a part of.
How should the attorney respond?
   A. Change his behavior in various ways to get the best possible outcome
   B. Mirror the client's behavior, becoming frustrated and aggressive
   C. Walk out of the meeting. If the client will not respect the attorney, then why should the attorney respect the client?
   D. None of the above

22. A very important resident of your village contacts your department and is upset about the way one of your co-workers handled the processing of his permit application.
Which of the following is the BEST way to move forward with this situation?
   A. Rush to respond to him right away as he is very important and busy
   B. Take responsibility for the mix-up and attempt to figure out how to appropriately fix the issue
   C. Attempt to see why he is so antagonistic and suggest he is part of the problem
   D. Make promises about fixing the issue as promptly as possible, even if you cannot actually keep the promise

23. An administrative assistant for the local police station receives a phone call from an angry resident. The assistant wants to aid in resolving the resident's issue and calm her down before she talks to an officer.
Which of the following steps should the assistant take while talking to the resident?
   A. Empathize
   B. Diagnose
   C. Apologize
   D. All of the above

24. After an ice storm passed through the area, the steps outside of Village Hall iced over. While an employee attempted to salt the area outside the building, a person slipped and fell as they were attempting to come in for a meeting.
How should this situation be handled?
   A. Start gathering evidence to prove that reasonable attempts were made to prevent injury for customers walking into the building
   B. Call insurance to get a claims adjustor out to the building as fast as possible to assist the person
   C. Get immediate medical attention for the person who is injured
   D. None of the above

25. A local customer of the park district tweets in his Twitter account poking fun at how slow and behind the times the park district is. After a week, the comments do not seem to stop.
Which of the following should the park district NOT do regarding the customer and his tweets?
    A. Directly contact the Twitter user to see what ways the park district could improve their slow process
    B. Before responding, check to ensure the response is professional and courteous
    C. Censor the Twitter account responsible for the tweet
    D. The park district should avoid doing all of the things mentioned above

25.____

KEY (CORRECT ANSWERS)

1.	B		11.	A
2.	A		12.	D
3.	C		13.	C
4.	D		14.	B
5.	A		15.	D
6.	C		16.	A
7.	D		17.	B
8.	B		18.	C
9.	B		19.	A
10.	C		20.	D

21. A
22. B
23. D
24. C
25. C

TEST 2

DIRECTIONS: Each question or incomplete statement is followed by several suggested answers or completions. Select the one that BEST answers the question or completes the statement. *PRINT THE LETTER OF THE CORRECT ANSWER IN THE SPACE AT THE RIGHT.*

1. Recently, the village mayor made controversial statements that angered many of the local residents. An employee at Village Hall has received a call from one of these angry people.
   How should she handle this situation?
   A. Deny any knowledge of the situation and explain that it is not her job to comment on the mayor's opinions
   B. Apologize and be transparent about what happened
   C. Give the person the mayor's phone number at Village Hall and explain they should be talking to the mayor
   D. Once the employee realizes what the phone call is about, she should see if there is any constructive criticism to bring to the mayor and promise to do so

   1.____

2. A local patron comes into the library and claims that he was charged for not returning a book that he says was returned to the drop box after the library was closed. The librarian knows that the patron never returned the book and is just trying to avoid paying the fine for a lost book.
   Which of the following statements should she make to the patron?
   A. "Sir, I know you're frustrated and I completely empathize. My goal is to help you sort this out."
   B. "Listen, I know you lost the book and you know you lost the book, so let's stop playing games and you can pay your fine if you wish to continue to check out books here."
   C. "Sir, I am so sorry that this happened! I know we'll get to the bottom of this – and that starts with your being honest about the book."
   D. "Sir, I tell you what. Do not worry about it. I am sure the book was returned and we just misplaced it. I'll wipe the fine and you can go ahead and check out any books you wish."

   2.____

3. A resident calls the park district fitness center to cancel her membership.
   What should the employee who receives the call do?
   A. Attempt to convince the resident to keep her membership by promoting the health benefits of an active lifestyle
   B. Keep the resident on the line and attempt to have her join another activity such as a league or tennis lessons
   C. Apologize that the fitness center could not fit her needs, cancel the membership, and ask what went wrong so the center can improve in the future.
   D. Cancel the membership and promptly hang up

   3.____

4. The local post office receives a phone call from an angry customer who wants to know why her package has not yet arrived. Upon checking the tracking for the package, the employee cannot determine where the package is.
How should he proceed?
   A. Apologize for the package not arriving on time
   B. Admit that as of right now the package cannot be located
   C. Explain the process for filing a claim on a missing or lost package
   D. All of the above

4._____

5. An IRS employee recently received training on how to comply with equality legislation when a customer calls asking for assistance on a tax issue they're having.
How should this recent training affect that phone call?
   A. Range of services will decrease   B. Service offer will be limited
   C. Fair service will be provided   D. Range of services will increase

5._____

6. A customer attempts to reach out to the Public Works Department of her local government via Twitter to ask a question about garbage collection. The Public Works main Twitter account informs the customer that she will need to contact the Garbage Collection Twitter account in order for her question to be answered. The customer is frustrated because of how long it is taking for her to receive a simple answer.
How could Public Works improve in the future to improve its social media customer service?
   A. Assess the need for multiple accounts for the department, as it could be better to have one social media platform with shared ownership between departments
   B. Educate each department's social media team on how to provide the best possible customer care via social media
   C. Ask customers to contact the department by more conventional means in order to better handle customer service
   D. Both A and B

6._____

7. An irate resident telephones a clerk who handles housing tax assessments for the town.
How should the clerk react so that the customer's expectations are met with a positive outcome?
   A. Follow the department's procedures for this kind of call
   B. Describe why the issue happened
   C. Urge the resident to be more patient since there are new members on department staff
   D. Support the department's position and tell the resident to submit his complaint in writing

7._____

8. A concerned citizen is following up on a report she made to Child and Youth Services two days ago.
What should the employee receiving the citizen's follow-up do to make sure the situation is handled effectively?

8._____

A. Issue the full report to the citizen
B. Express gratitude for filing a report and explain that Child and Youth Services takes it very seriously and is looking into the matter. Tell her that it is the policy of Child and Youth Services to not discuss open or closed investigations with citizens.
C. Explain to the citizen that the report has been filed and the situation has been taken care of, and that she should follow up with the child's family for specific details
D. None of the above

9. When a resident asks why Village Hall needs him to fill out an online survey he just received, what should the employee's explanation be?
    A. So organizational procedure changes can be avoided
    B. So changes can be made to ensure and maintain resident satisfaction
    C. So residents can be added to a list that informs of upcoming events
    D. So information can be gathered and shared with other organizations and departments

10. Someone walks into the local Health Department looking to talk to anyone who works there. The employee who helps her has no knowledge of the person or the meeting ahead of time.
    What question should the employee ask to help establish the person's needs?
    A. "Are you happy with how you've been treated so far?"
    B. "Would you be willing to fill out a survey after this to attest to the great care and service you received today?"
    C. "I would love to help you, but I do not know what you need yet."
    D. "Is there anything I can help you with today?"

11. A teenager who recently passed her driving test seems very nervous when she approaches the DMV employee who will process her request.
    What technique can the employee use to help put the teen at ease?
    A. Ask the teen to hurry up
    B. Avoid speaking to the teen beyond what is necessary to process her request as quickly and efficiently as possible
    C. Relate to the teen by reminiscing about the employee's own experience
    D. Have a younger, friendlier-looking co-worker help the teen. It may put her at ease if she is closer in age.

12. During a customer interaction at the post office, an employee asks for the customer's e-mail address. The customer wants to know why they need an e-mail address.
    The employee explains that he needs the e-mail address because
    A. it will help keep customers informed of service changes, delivery delays and other pertinent information
    B. it will help increase online sales revenue through discounts and promotional offerings
    C. it allows the post office to gain more information on its customers, which it shares with the federal government
    D. all of the above

13. A man comes into the state tollway office and asks to talk to a specific employee. When he meets the employee, the person is upset because he claims the employee promised to waive fees attached to his account, but the person just received a final notice that those fees needed to be paid or further action would be taken.
Knowing that he did make the promise, what should the employee do?
    A. Explain that the promise he made was overruled by his supervisor and that the customer must pay the fines
    B. Pretend like no promise was ever offered and tell the person he'll have to pay the fee
    C. Explain that the final notice must have been sent while the waived fees were processing, and confirm they have been removed from the account
    D. None of the above

13.____

14. A public service employee is meeting with a local customer who is upset with how his claim has been handled.
Which of the following should the employee AVOID doing if he wants the meeting to go well?
    A. Listen to the complaint and show empathy
    B. Take an important text/phone call during the meeting
    C. Tell the customer he will fix this issue together and solicit ideas from the customer about what he would be satisfied with
    D. Let the customer know that the employee will do everything possible to help the customer with what he needs

14.____

15. A woman walks into the post office with a damaged package she claims she received yesterday.
Which of the following should the employee NOT state to the woman during the ensuing conversation?
    A. "I am so sorry your product arrived damaged!"
    B. "I see your package was insured; would you like my assistance in filing an indemnity claim?"
    C. "I have had this happen to me before as well. I know how frustrated you are right now!"
    D. "Are you sure this is our fault? This doesn't look like shipping damage."

15.____

16. The university bookstore receives a complaint from a customer who claims she bought an item there yesterday and then found it went on clearance today. What should the employee who received the customer do?
    A. Ask for the customer's item and receipt to confirm the purchase date, then credit the difference back to the customer
    B. Explain that the customer can return the item, but cannot repurchase it in order to get the discount
    C. Speak with management to ensure a credit can be given and then give it to the customer, but add that this a one-time convenience
    D. Apologize for the frustration, but explain that policy does not allow for any returns or exchanges on clearance items

16.____

17. A dissatisfied resident engages Village Hall via Twitter to complain about the lack of quality in the road maintenance outside her house after a winter storm. How should the person in charge of social media respond to the resident's tweet?
    She should
    A. not respond, as Village Hall cannot fix every small problem and trying to respond will only call more attention to the issue
    B. tweet back for the resident to call Village Hall during normal operating hours in order to discuss the issue
    C. directly message the resident to find out why she was dissatisfied and attempt to gather feedback about a better process for fixing the issue
    D. mention the company that is contracted to handle road maintenance, so they can take care of the problem

17.____

18. An employee who is responsible for social media posts for the Parks and Recreation Department notices that a number of negative reviews recently posted about the department all seem to be made by the same online profile. After digging around, the employee determines that the profile belongs to someone who recently had a bad experience with one of the programs run by the department.
    What should the employee do?
    A. Call out the person by showing that their bad reviews are based off one experience
    B. Post a general statement about how the Parks and Recreation Department strives to give residents the best possible experience, and add that this particular resident is just "trolling"
    C. Ignore the comments and trust the public to know that one person posting negative reviews does not mean the department has a negative reputation
    D. Seek out the person privately and attempt to correct any wrongdoing on the part of the department

18.____

19. An employee for City Hall must meet with a group of concerned citizens for input on a potential City park project.
    How should the employee dress for this meeting?
    A. Dress casually because the meeting might take long
    B. Dress professionally to convey competence and ability to meet the citizens' needs
    C. Dress casually to put the citizens at ease during the meeting
    D. Dress professionally to intimidate the citizens and show superiority

19.____

20. A customer comes into the State Tollway Office and complains that he was given a defective sensor for electronic payment of tolls.
    Which of the following should the employee NOT do in his attempt to help resolve this situation?
    A. Give the customer personal contact information so he can contact the employee anytime there is an issue in the future
    B. Reimburse the customer with a new sensor

20.____

C. Compensate the customer by waiving any extra fees that may have incurred from the unprocessed tolls
D. Offer the customer a sincere apology for the inconvenience he's had to endure

21. A customer places a complicated order over the telephone.
What is the BEST way to ensure the details of the order are correct?
    A. Repeat the order over the telephone
    B. Record the telephone call
    C. Confirm the order in writing
    D. Take down the details in writing

21._____

22. There is a new initiative from Village Hall to promote a healthier lifestyle for residents, and part of the program launch features employees calling residents and then scheduling meetings to explain the initiative in greater detail. When one employee meets with a resident, the resident interrupts their original pitch and asks simply why they need to hear about the features and benefits of the program.
How should the employee respond?
    A. Kindly ask the resident to stop interrupting so he can explain everything
    B. Let the resident know that is how residents will understand what the program will do for them
    C. Explain that the village is putting such major emphasis on healthy lifestyles that it wants to discuss the benefits with residents in person
    D. Both B and C

22._____

23. A customer telephones the County Clerk's office complaining that her ADA rights are being violated because the handicapped parking space is not wide enough to accommodate her and her vehicle. The employee speaking to the customer knows that the parking space is the required 96 inches wide, but also knows that the size of a parking lot sometimes makes it difficult for customers to park correctly.
How should the employee handle this situation?
    A. Apologize to the customer and politely end the conversation. Then call the lawyer that represents the County for legal representation and counsel.
    B. Express empathy that the clerk's office is such a hassle for the customer, but explain that the building is ADA compliant. Offer to collaborate on a solution that will work for the customer.
    C. Call the customer out for being wrong. Offer to show her any forms of plans that show that the clerk's office is ADA compliant.
    D. Explain to the customer that she is right and the clerk's office will attempt to make their parking lot and handicapped spaces more compliant for the customer

23._____

24. A resident walks into the Homeowners' Association office and asks for the deadline to file an application to run for one of the offices of the HOA. The employee working does not know the answer.
What is the BEST way to respond to the resident's request?
   A. Tell the resident what she thinks the answer might be
   B. Refer the resident to a supervisor
   C. Inform the person that she does not know, but will find out as quickly as possible
   D. Explain that this kind of information is not something that can be given out to the public

24.____

25. A customer at the DMV asks an employee to do something that the employee cannot accommodate.
In responding to the request, the employee should AVOID doing which of the following?
   A. Quote DMV policy regarding the customer's request
   B. Explain to the customer why the employee cannot accommodate her request
   C. Make vague statements that allow for interpretation and, therefore, wiggle room
   D. Both A and C

25.____

KEY (CORRECT ANSWERS)

1.	B		11.	C
2.	A		12.	A
3.	C		13.	C
4.	D		14.	B
5.	C		15.	D
6.	D		16.	A
7.	A		17.	C
8.	B		18.	D
9.	B		19.	B
10.	D		20.	A

21. A
22. D
23. B
24. C
25. D

EXAMINATION SECTION

TEST 1

DIRECTIONS: Each question or incomplete statement is followed by several suggested answers or completions. Select the one that BEST answers the question or completes the statement. *PRINT THE LETTER OF THE CORRECT ANSWER IN THE SPACE AT THE RIGHT.*

1. Which of the following are covered under the definition of customer service? 1.____
   A. A positive environment set up to efficiently handle customer requests
   B. Infrastructure designed to distribute merchandise in a timely fashion
   C. Employees filling distinct roles to meet customer needs
   D. All of the above

2. An organization that has a clearly established customer service approach can distinguish itself from competitors. This is referred to as the organization's 2.____
   A. customer prioritization   B. service culture
   C. imagineering   D. none of the above

3. The physical space of a hospitality setting is MOST commonly referred to as the 3.____
   A. customer landscape   B. business policy
   C. servicescape   D. arena of service

4. When dealing with a customer, one must be knowledgeable, capable and enthusiastic when delivering products and/or services and it must be done in a manner that satisfies 4.____
   A. both identified and unidentified needs
   B. local and global competition
   C. quality and quantity of goods/services
   D. all demands of the customer

5. Employees at the center learn at their orientation that services are inseparable because service quality and customer satisfaction are largely dependent on which of the following? 5.____
   A. Interactions between employees and customers
   B. Uniform offerings for individuals
   C. Establishing patents for individual services
   D. All of the above

6. An organization with a strong customer service culture 6.____
   A. allows employees to use their own initiative to solve customer problems
   B. has policies that allow employees to easily please customers
   C. provides extensive customer service training for employees
   D. all of the above

7. Which of the following is TRUE of customer contact through electronic mail?
   A. Be sure to use all caps for important aspects of the e-mail
   B. State the purpose of the message clearly
   C. Do not feel the need to respond immediately
   D. Include lengthy descriptions in the body of the e-mail

8. A clerk is speaking to residents at a zoning committee meeting and uses the word "coulda" instead of "could have" in his presentation.
   This is an example of
   A. good enunciation   B. poor tone
   C. poor enunciation   D. proper pitch

9. An employee is delivering a presentation to parents about the benefits of children joining summer camps when someone complains that the employee's changing pitch makes it hard to hear what he is saying and that he needs to fix it.
   What does the parent mean by fixing his pitch?
   The employee needs to
   A. keep his voice from going too high or too low
   B. keep his voice from getting too soft or too loud
   C. keep his attitude towards certain subjects in check
   D. make sure his words are clearly spoken and not garbled

10. A clerk recently moved from answering phone calls every day to working face-to-face with residents.
    Which of the following will help her be most successful when transferring from phone to personal communication?
    A. Focus on sharing only positive information
    B. Speak more authoritatively
    C. Maintain a more casual tone and familiarity with residents
    D. Positive communication through eye contact and body language

11. Talking via telephone
    A. is less personal than sending an e-mail message
    B. is a poor way to reach most residents
    C. can allow residents to receive instant feedback
    D. is not popular within public services

12. An employee is in charge of calling local homeowners to tell them about upcoming activities, and more often than not she needs to leave a voicemail.
    Which of the following is the MOST effective way to leave voicemails?
    A. Be courteous
    B. Provide the appropriate information
    C. Contain lengthy details
    D. Both A and B

13. You are dealing with a parent who is upset about a miscommunication related to her child's application for an activity. Which of the following would be LEAST frustrating for the parent to hear from you?
    A. "I don't know. I will do my best."
    B. "Let me see what I can do for you."
    C. "I apologize, but you will have to…"
    D. "Oh, my manager should be able to help you, but he's not in right now."

14. If a part-time assistant employee should need to apologize to customers, which of the following should he NOT do when apologizing?
    A. Apologize right away
    B. Be sincere in his apology
    C. Make the apology personal
    D. Offer an official apology from the department

15. If a clerk's office is looking to improve its processes to increase community satisfaction, feedback received should be each of the following EXCEPT
    A. centered on internal customers
    B. ongoing
    C. available internally to everyone from employees to supervisors
    D. focused on a limited number of indicators

16. A member of the community has identified a flaw in one of the policies regarding town hall meetings. Now that the problem has been identified, all of the following should be steps toward resolving the issue EXCEPT
    A. following up on the problem resolution
    B. making whatever promises are necessary
    C. listening and responding to all complaints
    D. providing the resident with whatever was originally requested

17. When looking to achieve the best results as someone who interacts with the public, one should always strive to represent
    A. the entire organization
    B. the customer
    C. the department
    D. their direct supervisor

18. Approximately how long does it take a person on hold to become annoyed?
    A. 1 minute   B. 40 seconds   C. 20 seconds   D. 2 minutes

19. If an employee answers the phone and is asked to transfer the call to a co-worker, which of the following would be the MOST appropriate response?
    A. "She isn't in right now, so I'll have to take a message."
    B. "She's still at lunch. Can I take a message?"
    C. "She should be back soon. Could you call back in 15 minutes?"
    D. "Let me transfer you. If she's not in, please leave a message and she will return your call."

20. A public employee has been specifically assigned to deal with public complaints because he is remarkably skilled at dealing with residents. Which of the following mentalities would explain why the employee is so effective at dealing with residents?
    A. They always cave in to whatever demands the residents make
    B. They effectively manage residents' expectations
    C. They always sincerely apologize no matter who is at fault
    D. Both A and C

20.____

21. When dealing with a frustrated customer, which of the following practices should an employee avoid?
    A. Immediately offer a solution to their problem
    B. Soothe the customer's frustration first
    C. Remain positive and non-confrontational with the customer
    D. Let the customer vent and feel like they've shared their feelings accurately

21.____

22. The town clerk's office in Avondale is highly rated by town residents. When surveyed, residents of Avondale claim that their town clerks always have such great customer service.
    Of the customer service techniques listed below, which one is MOST likely the reason for such high ratings?
    A. When dealing with abusive residents, Avondale clerks always hang up on them
    B. Clerks in Avondale have a readied list of solutions to resident problems, so they are able to offer personalized solutions right away
    C. Avondale clerks always follow up with residents who call or come in
    D. Clerks always look customers in the eye even when they are frustrated and upset

22.____

23. If a parent was told there would be space in a day camp for all of her children, and only two of them ended up being placed together, which of the following actions would be PROPER for a parks employee to take?
    A. Offer a sincere apology and attempt to fix the problem
    B. Promise the parent that all her children will be together even if it means dropping other children from the camp
    C. Explain the Parks Department policy regarding camp sign-up and tell the parent to contact a manager for further explanation
    D. Tell the parent she needs to speak to someone with more authority

23.____

24. If a person has a hearing impairment, which of the following practical solutions could a clerk have in place to help them?
    A. Reading a description of policy to the person
    B. Write a note to answer a question they have
    C. Read the words communicated by the person's "communication board"
    D. Assist the person in maneuvering through the physical space of the office

24.____

25. When dealing with a call, who should end the phone call first?
    A. The person who answered
    B. The person who called
    C. Either one – it doesn't matter
    D. A manager

25.____

KEY (CORRECT ANSWERS)

1. D
2. B
3. C
4. A
5. A

6. D
7. B
8. C
9. A
10. D

11. C
12. D
13. B
14. D
15. A

16. B
17. A
18. C
19. D
20. B

21. A
22. C
23. A
24. B
25. B

TEST 2

DIRECTIONS: Each question or incomplete statement is followed by several suggested answers or completions. Select the one that BEST answers the question or completes the statement. *PRINT THE LETTER OF THE CORRECT ANSWER IN THE SPACE AT THE RIGHT.*

1. Which of the following would be considered acceptable for an office clerk when answering the phone?
     A. Chewing gum
     B. Listening to music
     C. Eating a snack while on mute
     D. Wearing a headset

     1.____

2. Why would asking a caller for their phone number be important?
     A. In case they get disconnected
     B. To show them you are polite and considerate
     C. In case the caller is rude, this way you can call them back
     D. For future instances where calling residents back might make sense

     2.____

3. When rolling out a new program to help train employees in better customer service, the manager starts off by talking about the importance of telephone greetings.
   Why is this so important?
     A. It is the first impression the customer has of the department
     B. It shows the customer that employees are happy
     C. It shows that you are polite
     D. It isn't that important, but the manager thinks it is

     3.____

4. Which of the following is the MOST important aspect of an employee's voice in a telephone call?
     A. Their volume
     B. Their speed
     C. Their tone
     D. All of these aspects are equally important

     4.____

5. A clerk is on the phone with a customer when another customer walks into the building.
   If the clerk must put the caller on hold, what do they need to say or ask?
     A. "Would you like to be put on hold?"
     B. "I apologize for the inconvenience, but please hold."
     C. "Would it be OK if I put you on hold for a moment?"
     D. "I have to let you go. Please call back later."

     5.____

6. When a resident comes into your office for a face-to-face meeting, it is of increased importance that you communicate positively with your
     A. words
     B. body language
     C. tone
     D. none of the above

     6.____

7. A customer calls when employees are at an all-staff meeting. When calling the customer back, a clerk reaches their voicemail.
   Which of the following information is the MOST important to leave?
   A. The date and time
   B. Ask them to call back
   C. The employee's telephone number
   D. Apologize repeatedly for missing their call

8. If an employee is in the middle of a conversation about town hall policy with a co-worker and the phone rings, what should the employee do?
   A. Get caller's information and call back after the conversation is finished
   B. Tell the co-worker to wait until finished with the phone call
   C. Answer the call and put caller on hold until conversation is finished
   D. Answer the call and transfer it to another employee who is not currently busy

9. When dealing with a resident who casually uses vulgar language, it is MOST appropriate for a town employee to
   A. tell the resident to come back when he learns how to speak
   B. converse with the resident using equally coarse language
   C. politely ask the resident to refrain from using vulgar language
   D. make the resident wait longer so he knows it won't be tolerated

10. The mayor's office has recently come under fire for a variety of perceived scandals.
    In this emergency situation, which of the following would NOT be a recommended step in handling the crisis?
    A. Minimizing damage to the office's reputation through whatever means necessary
    B. Taking responsibility and apologizing
    C. Providing constant updates on the situation
    D. Designating one spokesperson to handle the relaying of updates

11. A resident complains that recreation center employees are using bureaucratic or overly technical communication. This type of language is often referred to as
    A. clichés   B. jargon   C. euphemisms   D. legalese

12. Which of the following strategies does an employee need to utilize to convince the public to believe a message that is contrary to their beliefs?
    A. Cognitive dissonance   B. Uses and gratification
    C. Sleeper effect   D. Source credibility

13. When communicating with parents of a summer camp run by the district, which of the following should NOT be a goal of the process?
    A. Motivation   B. Persuasion
    C. Mutual understanding   D. Isolation of the conflict

14. A manager comes up with a new procedure that he believes would improve the claims process that residents need to go through. Some employees agree that the procedure would make sense and others do not. One employee openly criticizes the idea to the manager.
Which of the following actions should the manager take?
He should
    A. meet with the employee for a talk and explain why bypassing his authority is unacceptable
    B. not respond to the critics in order to avoid unnecessary risks
    C. reprimand the employee who went over his head
    D. only implement the procedures that all agreed were good in order to satisfy employees

15. The county clerk's office is working on improving its employees' professionalism.
If employees are attempting to maintain a professional demeanor, what should they NOT do after making a mistake?
    A. Work to do better at the next opportunity
    B. Move on
    C. Accept responsibility
    D. Explain or rationalize the error

16. According to most recent surveys, data reveals that most white-collar workers
    A. have about a 25 percent efficiency rate when listening
    B. lose only about 25 percent efficiency when listening
    C. never take listening for granted
    D. learn to listen effectively since hearing is the important active learned process

17. Which of the following are NOT one of the four phases of listening to a customer?
    A. Hearing   B. Translating   C. Responding   D. Comprehending

18. Which of the following societal factors might impact a resident/employee interaction?
    A. Increased efficiency in technology
    B. Globalization of the economy
    C. More people between the ages of 16-24 entering the workplace
    D. Geopolitical changes

19. If a resident comes in confused about a policy change, which of the following approaches should an employee take to handle the situation?
    A. Communicate negatively when they need to
    B. Avoid gestures such as smiling or looking at customers when speaking to them
    C. Recognize how they tend to communicate and adjust accordingly if the customer is still showing signs of confusion
    D. Understand that many people are doubtful of good customer service

20. In order to avoid negative public perception, which of the following "finger pointing" words/phrases should be avoided when interacting with the public?
    A. Let me   B. You   C. Why   D. Yes

21. In an effort to improve government/resident relations, the mayor wants to roll out a new PR format that stresses public communication.
    Which of the following strategies should NOT be suggested as part of the PR campaign?
    A. Plan the message
    B. Greet residents warmly
    C. Listen carefully and respond appropriately
    D. Let the residents initiate conversations

22. A resident complains that the department does not always treat the local residents as people.
    Of the following, which would be the BEST strategy for resolving this issue?
    A. Accept responsibility and offer specific assistance
    B. Blame the customer when necessary
    C. Provide policies as reasons for actions
    D. None of the above

23. When providing feedback to residents, which of the following strategies is NOT effective?
    A. Remain emotional when providing feedback
    B. Confirm residents' meaning before offering feedback
    C. Ensure the feedback is appropriate to the original message
    D. Avoid extreme criticism or negative language

24. An employee at City Hall receives special treatment from his manager. This causes the employee to feel empowered, which then leads to him abusing authority and power.
    Which of the following would MOST likely happen if this behavior is allowed to continue?
    A. Other employees would begin to feel empowered
    B. Co-workers would work harder to demonstrate their commitment
    C. Residents would begin to work with the empowered employee because he would be able to get things done
    D. The rest of the department would start to feel resentment and frustration, and might potentially retaliate

25. If a town clerk works well with customers on the phone but struggles with face-to-face interactions, which of the following might BEST explain the problem?
    A. The actual words the clerk uses   B. Facial and other body cues
    C. Vocal cues   D. Both A and C

KEY (CORRECT ANSWERS)

1.	D		11.	B
2.	A		12.	A
3.	A		13.	D
4.	D		14.	A
5.	C		15.	D
6.	B		16.	A
7.	C		17.	B
8.	B		18.	C
9.	C		19.	C
10.	A		20.	B

21. D
22. A
23. A
24. D
25. B

TEST 3

DIRECTIONS: Each question or incomplete statement is followed by several suggested answers or completions. Select the one that BEST answers the question or completes the statement. *PRINT THE LETTER OF THE CORRECT ANSWER IN THE SPACE AT THE RIGHT.*

1. If an employee's body position is causing customers to feel she is projecting a mood/attitude that she isn't actually expressing, what does the employee need to work on improving?
   A. Pitch	B. Articulation	C. Posture	D. Inflection

   1._____

2. A newly hired assistant notices that everyone in his department has received a new computer system except for him.
   What should he do?
   A. Assume this is a mistake and speak to his manager
   B. Complain to H.R.
   C. Quit
   D. Confront his manager regarding his unfair treatment

   2._____

3. A team leader in your department notices that ample amounts of department-labeled property have come up missing in recent weeks. The leader notices a fellow supervisor putting stationery and other equipment into a personal bag on a few different occasions and believes this person is responsible.
   What is the LEAST effective response to the situation?
   A. Gather more evidence to catch the person in the act
   B. Do nothing – if guilty, someone else will likely catch the colleague
   C. Privately ask other colleagues if they've noticed anything suspicious recently
   D. Inform a supervisor higher up in the organization that this person is a potential suspect

   3._____

4. Near the end of the work day, an official advisor accidentally sends an e-mail containing confidential information to the wrong person.
   Which of the following would be the BEST thing for the advisor to do?
   A. Overlook the error. Send the e-mail to the correct person and leave things as they are.
   B. Find a senior advisor and explain the mistake and have them deal with the problem
   C. Leave the office and deal with any fallout tomorrow
   D. Immediately send a follow-up e-mail to the "wrong" person explaining the mistake. Then send the e-mail to the correct person.

   4._____

5. If an employee is engaged with a customer and no one else is around when the phone rings, what is the PROPER step to take in this situation?
   A. Let the phone ring and continue to work with the customer in person
   B. Take the call and address the caller's issue, then hang up and come back to the customer
   C. Ask the customer to answer the phone while trying to resolve their issue.
   D. Tell the customer "excuse me" while answering the phone, then put the caller on hold while going back to the customer

5.____

6. According to many national retailer surveys, what do consumers remember the MOST about their customer service experience?
   A. The cost of the merchandise/experience
   B. The demeanor of the employee who engaged them
   C. The cleanliness of the office/area
   D. How nice the employees were

6.____

7. When attempting to help a resident make a decision about programs offered by your agency, it is important to remember that the majority of purchasing decisions consumers make are based upon
   A. what they think
   B. a potential free gift
   C. how they feel
   D. all of the above

7.____

8. In an effort to improve procedures in your department, a memo has been sent to employees. In it, one highlighted section focuses on the importance of avoiding closed-ended questions/comments.
   Following the advice of the memo, which question/comment should an employee avoid stating to a resident?
   A. "Can I help you?"
   B. "What is it you would like to see accomplished?"
   C. "So the challenges you've faced so far are..."
   D. "How would you like to see that improved?"

8.____

9. Numerous surveys indicate that consumers would actually pay more for
   A. self-checkout machines
   B. free product/demonstration giveaways
   C. more streamlined customer service
   D. apps using customer-service bots

9.____

10. Which of the following is an example of a proper "Activation Greeting"?
    A. "My name is _____. Let me tell you about our programs."
    B. "How many are there in your group?"
    C. "Hi! Welcome to _____."
    D. Both A and C

10.____

11. When interacting with members of the public, which of the following is the MOST important thing to do?
    A. Ask them to pay for services up front
    B. Smile at them
    C. Learn their name and call them by it
    D. Ask questions

12. Which of the following pieces of advice would help a clerk the MOST when working with the public?
    A. Pay attention to needs of others and offer only general solutions
    B. Hear what others are saying but do not take their comments to heart
    C. Focus on efficiency of service over quality of service
    D. Clearly understand the motives and needs of others

13. A member of the community complains that counselors at her child's camp do not listen to what she is telling them.
    Which technique listed below would improve understanding between the two parties?
    A. Reflective listening
    B. Narrow selections
    C. Reflective thinking
    D. Valid suggestions

14. When dealing with elderly residents, which of the following facts should be considered by a public official?
    A. They expect to be treated with courtesy and respect
    B. Expect them to avoid eye contact
    C. They prefer the telephone to personal contact
    D. They expect text and e-mail over face-to-face communication

15. If you are hired as a camp counselor for younger residents, it is important to remember all of the following about their behavior EXCEPT that they
    A. value technology
    B. are used to multitasking and access to instant information
    C. make less eye contact
    D. prefer more formal interactions

16. If one is trying to improve morale regarding customer/worker relations, which of the following is NOT a recommended thing to do?
    A. Publicly embarrass customers who are rude to the office employees
    B. Greet the customer with "Good Morning"
    C. Politely ask customers who cut in line to wait until it is their turn
    D. Thank customers for doing business with you

17. When hired by a public office, which of the following would be part of the newly hired employee's performance code?
    A. Report on time in a calm and controlled manner
    B. Present oneself in a neat and clean way
    C. Treat co-workers and residents with dignity and respect
    D. All of the above

18. If an employee sometimes "bends the rules" to honor a request from a customer, what service concept would explain this action?
    A. Motivated marketing strategy
    B. Power selling philosophy
    C. Employee empowerment
    D. Selling out for the customer

18.____

19. A Parks and Recreation worker is attempting to improve relations with the groups who sign up for his arts and crafts program.
    He should remember all of the following "Customer Service Rules" EXCEPT
    A. Customer service has a large effect on customer satisfaction
    B. Modern consumers are already more satisfied with customer service today than ever before
    C. Modern consumers have many different mechanisms by which to complain
    D. Feeling empowered as an employee usually leads to higher customer satisfaction

19.____

20. A marketing executive employee wishes to emphasize customer loyalty. Which of the following marketing strategies should the employee focus on when working with customers?
    A. Relationship marketing
    B. Undercover marketing
    C. Diversity marketing
    D. Transactional marketing

20.____

21. Why would a campaign manager for an elected official be interested in conducting a mail survey over other methods of surveying?
    It would
    A. avoid non-response problems
    B. speed up the process by which surveys are returned to them
    C. avoid participation by incorrect respondents
    D. enable the completion of the survey at a convenient time

21.____

22. At the end of each session, a counselor takes it upon herself to conduct research on the effectiveness of the program. She is worried that respondents won't be truthful, so she decides that the BEST way to avoid bias would be to conduct a(n) _____ survey.
    A. personal   B. telephone   C. internet   D. observational

22.____

23. A resident walks into the office and submits an application. When she is given additional forms to complete, she grumbles about "bureaucratic red tape" and how it's slowing down her application approval.
    How should an employee handle this situation?
    A. Be patient with the resident but do not explain the reason for the forms
    B. Tell the resident why the additional forms are necessary
    C. Suggest that the resident take it up with the manager if she wants the policy changed
    D. Say that the application will not be processed until ALL forms are completed

23.____

24. An employee's next-door neighbor has been hired as summer help, which the employee knows about because he has to type a confidential letter from the director to human resources about the hire. The neighbor does not yet know of the hiring decision, and the employee will see the neighbor later that day. Which one of the following should the employee do? 24.____
    A. Say nothing and wait for the offer to become official
    B. Congratulate the neighbor confidentially
    C. Inform a handful of people including the neighbor's close friends
    D. None of the above

25. A child with vision impairment wants to join a summer day camp and is denied access because the camp focuses on games and activities in which sight is required. If the parent comes in and complains to you, which of the following actions should you take and why? 25.____
    A. Modify the camp so the child can join because it is bad publicity to deny a child with a disability
    B. Offer another camp that does not focus on so many "sight-based" activities at a reduced rate so the parent and child do not feel left out
    C. Enroll the child and ensure they are allowed to participate in a meaningful way, because it's against the law to prevent the child from signing up
    D. Tell the parent they can talk to a supervisor because you have no authority to change the decision

---

KEY (CORRECT ANSWERS)

1.	C		11.	B
2.	A		12.	D
3.	B		13.	A
4.	D		14.	A
5.	D		15.	D
6.	B		16.	A
7.	C		17.	D
8.	A		18.	C
9.	C		19.	B
10.	C		20.	A

21.	D
22.	C
23.	B
24.	A
25.	C

TEST 4

DIRECTIONS: Each question or incomplete statement is followed by several suggested answers or completions. Select the one that BEST answers the question or completes the statement. *PRINT THE LETTER OF THE CORRECT ANSWER IN THE SPACE AT THE RIGHT.*

1. If a customer tells an employee they need to work on having open body language, which of the following would be an example?
 A. Fiddling
 B. Minimal eye contact
 C. Folded arms
 D. Frequent hand gestures

1.____

2. As a phone operator for the bureau director's office, it is important that you make the constituents feel as though you are actively listening to their concerns.
 What is the MOST effective way to demonstrate this?
 A. Use affirmation with words like "ok", "yes" and "I understand"
 B. Interrupt with your own thoughts
 C. Ask numerous closed questions
 D. Talk over the constituent

2.____

3. When a resident walks up to a clerk's desk, which of the following is the BEST way to greet them?
 A. Wave
 B. Ask them what they need
 C. Welcome them and ask how they can be helped
 D. Ignore them until finished with the current task

3.____

4. When a customer complains through e-mail, an office clerk should
 A. forward the e-mail to a supervisor
 B. reply right away with a potential solution
 C. share the complaint via the office's official Twitter handle
 D. reply right away with a hurried answer

4.____

5. Interacting with the public is a constant back and forth where feedback is essential to improving service.
 Which of the following methods would be BEST to obtain feedback from the public?
 A. Cold calling
 B. Tweeting
 C. Survey via website
 D. Ask the staff what they think

5.____

6. If residents continually complain that clerks do not truly understand what they are trying to tell them, which of the following practices might help improve this communication barrier?
 A. Paraphrasing
 B. Encoding
 C. Rapport building
 D. Decoding

6.____

2 (#4)

7. A customer complains to an employee and demands to see a supervisor. The employee is not sure to who to direct this angry customer. Which of the following methods of illustrating hierarchy of the company would help the employee out?
    A. Diagramming
    B. Negotiation
    C. Brainstorming
    D. Organizational charts

7._____

8. A village clerk and a resident have a strong disagreement about how an office policy applies to their situation. A co-worker is asked to weigh in on the situation. How should the co-worker handle the situation?
    A. Take the employee's side since they have to work side by side
    B. Try to help both parties walk away feeling like they got what they wanted
    C. Take the resident's side since the office cannot afford bad publicity
    D. Have a supervisor intervene – it's better to pass responsibility onto someone in power

8._____

9. A parent accuses your department of making generalizations about their child based on the group to which they belong. Which of the following unfair, but common, ideas is the department being accused of?
    A. Racism
    B. Stereotyping
    C. Confirmation bias
    D. Rationale judgment

9._____

10. When a resident calls a government office, they expect the phone to be picked up by the _____ ring otherwise they feel as though their call is unimportant.
    A. 1st   B. 4th   C. 3rd   D. 7th

10._____

11. When working directly with a consumer on the phone or in person, which of the following would be considered inappropriate?
    A. Eating, drinking or chewing gum
    B. Speaking slowly and enunciating clearly
    C. Asking permission to put someone on hold
    D. Wearing a headset

11._____

12. Someone calls village hall and is extremely upset by a policy change enacted in the last board meeting. They demand an explanation that the clerk does not have. As the clerk tries to find the answer, how often should she update the angry caller on the status of the complaint (even if the clerk has no answer)?
    A. 2-3 minutes
    B. 35 seconds
    C. 1 minute
    D. Do not update them until an answer has been found

12._____

13. A resident is irate over how a co-worker of yours handled his claim process and now you have to handle his appeal. Throughout the process of filling out the necessary paperwork, this resident continues to not only berate the co-worker, but also starts complaining about how slow you are.
In this stressful situation, why is it important to stay calm and not let the resident get to you?
    A. They could be having a bad day and your anger may make the situation worse
    B. You need to show the resident you are willing to take the time necessary to resolve his or her problem
    C. They might be violent and could end up hurting you
    D. Both A and B

13.____

14. An employee is calling residents to thank them for volunteering for a food drive. As the employee moves through his list, he accidentally dials the wrong number, and a person on the other line answers.
What should the employee do?
    A. Apologize to the person for calling the wrong number
    B. Thank the person anyway
    C. Hang up before the person says anything else
    D. Try to sign the person up for the next food drive

14.____

15. Which of the following questions tell the customer that the employee wants to ensure that every need has been met before the interaction is over?
    A. "You've said everything you need to say, right?"
    B. "Is there anything else I can help you with?"
    C. "How can I help you today?"
    D. "Would you like me to transfer you to someone else?"

15.____

16. An elderly resident calls your department, but was trying to reach the Health and Sanitation Department. What should you do?
    A. Be polite
    B. Hastily transfer the person to the correct department
    C. Try to determine who they need to speak to and transfer them to that person directly if possible
    D. Both A and C

16.____

17. Which of the following would NOT be considered an example of good customer service?
    A. A parent waits three minutes to pick up their child from an after-school activity
    B. A clearly defined resolution process is in place for residents who have disagreements with public officials
    C. There is no line at the DMV, and a person waits 10 minutes before being serviced
    D. The park's pools briefly close at noon and 4 p.m. so they can be skimmed and checked for debris

17.____

18. A resident is angry about a zoning issue that prevents him from adding on to his garage.
    When dealing with this customer, which of the following should an employee NOT do?
    A. Acknowledge their emotion
    B. Ask questions
    C. Avoid escalating the argument
    D. Agree that the code is silly

18.____

19. A resident comes into the office where you work and complains that he was screened out of a job because of a vision impairment. He asks if this is legal and what he should do.
    You tell him it is not against the Americans With Disabilities Act if the employer screens him because
    A. clients prefer not to be served by the disabled
    B. a business cannot make a reasonable accommodation to work tasks for a specific disability
    C. co-workers dislike working with the disabled
    D. none of the above; ADA prevents any kind of "screening out" of disabled persons

19.____

20. During holidays and special events, the school office can sometimes be short-staffed, which requires all employees to know the different roles within the office. Some parents do not like when certain staff members act as the receptionist and those staff members do not like being the receptionist.
    Since both sides do not like the employees in that role, the employees should
    A. learn the receptionist's job and fill in when needed, but tell the principal that they, and parents, would prefer that they work in a different area
    B. tell the principal they don't want to work as a receptionist and ask to be excused from that role
    C. learn the receptionist's job, but when asked to fill in ask someone else to do it
    D. ask the principal to excuse then from the training, and explain that other employees who the parents like more could fill in for them

20.____

21. In an attempt to promote the recreation center in a positive light, which of the following advertising strategies would be MOST credible to town residents?
    A. Employees telling people how great the recreation center environment is
    B. Have local celebrities endorse the recreation center as the place to be
    C. Use current satisfied customers by having them "spread the word" about the recreation center
    D. Offer incredible discounts to the first 25 new customers to sign up

21.____

22. When a clerk is tasked with setting up a Town Hall meeting, all of the following are important EXCEPT
    A. spreading the word
    B. having an audience-selected moderator
    C. setting and following a schedule
    D. keeping things moving

22.____

23. A librarian works in the computer lab and a patron comes to her and says, "My flash drive is full. I need to save the document I just created. Where can I get a new flash drive?"
How should the librarian respond?
    A. Offer to help the patron e-mail the document to himself and then show him how to do it
    B. Ask the patron what he needs to save and then save it to a "Google Document" for them
    C. Offer him the use of a library-owned flash drive on the promise that he will bring it back
    D. Direct him to the nearest computer/retail store to purchase the flash drive

24. If people call for a Town Hall meeting, which of the following would NOT be a good reason to hold one?
    A. To voice a common concern shared by members of the community
    B. To present a new proposal that impacts the public
    C. To settle a dispute between rival advisors at City Hall
    D. To collect feedback in response to a new rule or policy implementation

25. Of the following Town Hall meeting pitfalls, which would MOST leave residents feeling as though they wasted their time?
    A. Not participative or interactive
    B. Poorly designed PowerPoint or on-screen presentation
    C. Poor time management
    D. Meaningless or irrelevant content

KEY (CORRECT ANSWERS)

1.	D	11.	A
2.	A	12.	C
3.	C	13.	D
4.	B	14.	A
5.	C	15.	B
6.	A	16.	D
7.	D	17.	C
8.	B	18.	D
9.	B	19.	B
10.	C	20.	A

21.	C
22.	B
23.	A
24.	C
25.	D

EXAMINATION SECTION
TEST 1

DIRECTIONS: Each question or incomplete statement is followed by several suggested answers or completions. Select the one that BEST answers the question or completes the statement. *PRINT THE LETTER OF THE CORRECT ANSWER IN THE SPACE AT THE RIGHT.*

1. In public agencies, communications should be based PRIMARILY on a 1.____
   A. two-way flow from the top down and from the bottom up, most of which should be given in writing to avoid ambiguity
   B. multi-direction flow among all levels and with outside persons
   C. rapid, internal one-way flow from the top down
   D. two-way flow of information, most of which should be given orally for purposes of clarity

2. In some organizations, changes in policy or procedures are often communicated by word of mouth from supervisors to employees with no prior discussion or exchange of viewpoints with employees. 2.____
   This procedure often produces employee dissatisfaction CHIEFLY because
   A. information is mostly unusable since a considerable amount of time is required to transmit information
   B. lower-level supervisors tend to be excessively concerned with minor details
   C. management has failed to seek employees' advice before making changes
   D. valuable staff time is lost between decision-making and the implementation of decisions

3. For good letter writing, you should try to visualize the person to whom you are writing, especially if you know him. 3.____
   Of the following rules, it is LEAST helpful in such visualization to think of
   A. the person's likes and dislikes, his concerns, and his needs
   B. what you would be likely to say if speaking in person
   C. what you would expect to be asked if speaking in person
   D. your official position in order to be certain that your words are proper

4. One approach to good informal letter writing is to make letters and conversational. 4.____
   All of the following practices will usually help to do this EXCEPT:
   A. If possible, use a style which is similar to the style used when speaking
   B. Substitute phrases for single words (e.g., *at the present time for now*)
   C. Use contractions of words (e.g., *you're* for *you are*)
   D. Use ordinary vocabulary when possible

5. All of the following rules will aid in producing clarity in report-writing EXCEPT:
   A. Give specific details or examples, if possible
   B. Keep related words close together in each sentence
   C. Present information in sequential order
   D. Put several thoughts or ideas in each paragraph

6. The one of the following statements about public relations which is MOST accurate is that
   A. in the long run, appearance gains better results than performance
   B. objectivity is decreased if outside public relations consultants are employed
   C. public relations is the responsibility of every employee
   D. public relations should be based on a formal publicity program

7. The form of communication which is usually considered to be MOST personally directed to the intended recipient is the
   A. brochure   B. film   C. letter   D. radio

8. In general, a document that presents an organization's views or opinions on a particular topic is MOST accurately known as a
   A. tear sheet   B. position paper
   C. flyer   D. journal

9. Assume that you have been asked to speak before an organization of persons who oppose a newly announced program in which you are involved. You feel tense about talking to this group.
   Which of the following rules generally would be MOST useful in gaining rapport when speaking before the audience?
   A. Impress them with your experience
   B. Stress all areas of disagreement
   C. Talk to the group as to one person
   D. Use formal grammar and language

10. An organization must have an effective public relations program since, at its best, public relations is a bridge to change.
    All of the following statements about communication and human behavior have validity EXCEPT:
    A. People are more likely to talk about controversial matters with like-minded people than with those holding other views
    B. The earlier an experience, the more powerful its effect since it influences how later experiences will be interpreted
    C. In periods of social tension, official sources gain increased believability
    D. Those who are already interested in a topic are the ones who are most open to receive new communications about it

11. An employee should be encouraged to talk easily and frankly when he is dealing with his supervisor.
In order to encourage such free communication, it would be MOST appropriate for a supervisor to behave in a(n)
    A. sincere manner; assure the employee that you will deal with him honestly and openly
    B. official manner; you are a supervisor and must always act formally with subordinates
    C. investigative manner; you must probe and question to get to a basis of trust
    D. unemotional manner; the employee's emotions and background should play no part in your dealings with him

12. Research findings show that an increase in free communication within an agency GENERALLY results in which one of the following?
    A. Improved morale and productivity
    B. Increased promotional opportunities
    C. An increase in authority
    D. A spirit of honesty

13. Assume that you are a supervisor and your superiors have given you a new-type procedure to be followed.
Before passing this information on to your subordinates, the one of the following actions that you should take FIRST is to
    A. ask your superiors to send out a memorandum to the entire staff
    B. clarify the procedure in your own mind
    C. set up a training course to provide instruction on the new procedure
    D. write a memorandum to your subordinates

14. Communication is necessary for an organization to be effective.
The one of the following which is LEAST important for most communication systems is that
    A. messages are sent quickly and directly to the person who needs them to operate
    B. information should be conveyed understandably and accurately
    C. the method used to transmit information should be kept secret so that security can be maintained
    D. senders of messages must know how their messages are received and acted upon

15. Which one of the following is the CHIEF advantage of listening willingly to subordinates and encouraging them to talk freely and honestly?
It
    A. reveals to supervisors the degree to which ideas that are passed down are accepted by subordinates
    B. reduces the participation of subordinates in the operation of the department
    C. encourages subordinates to try for promotion
    D. enables supervisors to learn more readily what the *grapevine* is saying

16. A supervisor may be informed through either oral or written reports. 16.____
Which one of the following is an ADVANTAGE of using oral reports?
    A. There is no need for a formal record of the report.
    B. An exact duplicate of the report is not easily transmitted to others.
    C. A good oral report requires little time for preparation.
    D. An oral report involves two-way communication between a subordinate and his supervisor.

17. Of the following, the MOST important reason why supervisors should 17.____
communicate effectively with the public is to
    A. improve the public's understanding of information that is important for them to know
    B. establish a friendly relationship
    C. obtain information about the kinds of people who come to the agency
    D. convince the public that services are adequate

18. Supervisors should generally NOT use phrases like *too hard, too easy*, and 18.____
a lot PRINCIPALLY because such phrases
    A. may be offensive to some minority groups
    B. are too informal
    C. mean different things to different people
    D. are difficult to remember

19. The ability to communicate clearly and concisely is an important element in 19.____
effective leadership.
Which of the following statements about oral and written communication is GENERALLY true?
    A. Oral communication is more time-consuming.
    B. Written communication is more likely to be misinterpreted.
    C. Oral communication is useful only in emergencies.
    D. Written communication is useful mainly when giving information to fewer than twenty people.

20. Rumors can often have harmful and disruptive effects on an organization. 20.____
Which one of the following is the BEST way to prevent rumors from becoming a problem?
    A. Refuse to act on rumors, thereby making them less believable.
    B. Increase the amount of information passed along by the *grapevine*.
    C. Distribute as much factual information as possible.
    D. Provide training in report writing.

21. Suppose that a subordinate asks you about a rumor he has heard. The rumor 21.____
deals with a subject which your superiors consider *confidential*.
Which of the following BEST describes how you should answer the subordinate? Tell

A. the subordinate that you don't make the rules and that he should speak to higher ranking officials
B. the subordinate that you will ask your superior for information
C. him only that you cannot comment on the matter
D. him the rumor is not true

22. Supervisors often find it difficult to *get their message across* when instructing newly appointed employees in their various duties.
The MAIN reason for this is generally that the
    A. duties of the employees have increased
    B. supervisor is often so expert in his area that he fails to see it from the learner's point of view
    C. supervisor adapts his instruction to the slowest learner in the group
    D. new employees are younger, less concerned with job security and more interested in fringe benefits

23. Assume that you are discussing a job problem with an employee under your supervision. During the discussion, you see that the man's eyes are turning away from you and that he is not paying attention.
In order to get the man's attention, you should FIRST
    A. ask him to look you in the eye
    B. talk to him about sports
    C. tell him he is being very rude
    D. change your tone of voice

24. As a supervisor, you may find it necessary to conduct meetings with your subordinates.
Of the following, which would be MOST helpful in assuring that a meeting accomplishes the purpose for which it was called?
    A. Give notice of the conclusions you would like to reach at the start of the meeting.
    B. Delay the start of the meeting until everyone is present.
    C. Write down points to be discussed in proper sequence.
    D. Make sure everyone is clear on whatever conclusions have been reached and on what must be done after the meeting.

25. Every supervisor will occasionally be called upon to deliver a reprimand to a subordinate. If done properly, this can greatly help an employee improve his performance.
Which one of the following is NOT a good practice to follow when giving a reprimand?
    A. Maintain your composure and temper
    B. Reprimand a subordinate in the presence of other employees so they can learn the same lesson
    C. Try to understand why the employee was not able to perform satisfactorily
    D. Let your knowledge of the man involved determine the exact nature of the reprimand

KEY (CORRECT ANSWERS)

1.	C		11.	A
2.	B		12.	A
3.	D		13.	B
4.	B		14.	C
5.	D		15.	A
6.	C		16.	D
7.	C		17.	A
8.	B		18.	C
9.	C		19.	B
10.	C		20.	C

21. B
22. B
23. D
24. D
25. B

TEST 2

DIRECTIONS: Each question or incomplete statement is followed by several suggested answers or completions. Select the one that BEST answers the question or completes the statement. *PRINT THE LETTER OF THE CORRECT ANSWER IN THE SPACE AT THE RIGHT.*

1. Usually one thinks of communication as a single step, essentially that of transmitting an idea.
   Actually, however, this is only part of a total process, the FIRST step of which should be
   A. the prompt dissemination of the idea to those who may be affected by it
   B. motivating those affected to take the required action
   C. clarifying the idea in one's own mind
   D. deciding to whom the idea is to be communicated

2. Research studies on patterns of informal communication have concluded that most individuals in a group tend to be passive recipients of news, while a few make it their business to spread it around in an organization.
   With this conclusion in mind, it would be MOST correct for the supervisor to attempt to identify these few individuals and
   A. give them the complete facts on important matters in advance of others
   B. inform the other subordinates of the identity of these few individuals so that their influence may be minimized
   C. keep them straight on the facts on important matters
   D. warn them to cease passing along any information to others

3. The one of the following which is the PRINCIPAL advantage of making an oral report is that it
   A. affords an immediate opportunity for two-way communication between the subordinate and superior
   B. is an easy method for the superior to use in transmitting information to others of equal rank
   C. saves the time of all concerned
   D. permits more precise pinpointing of praise or blame by means of follow-up questions by the superior

4. An agency may sometimes undertake a public relations program of a defensive nature.
   With reference to the use of defensive public relations, it would be MOST correct to state that it
   A. is bound to be ineffective since defensive statements, even though supported by factual data, can never hope to even partly overcome the effects of prior unfavorable attacks
   B. proves that the agency has failed to establish good relationships with newspapers, radio stations, or other means of publicity

C. shows that the upper echelons of the agency have failed to develop sound public relations procedures and techniques
D. is sometimes required to aid morale by protecting the agency from unjustified criticism and misunderstanding of policies or procedures

5. Of the following factors which contribute to possible undesirable public attitudes towards an agency, the one which is MOST susceptible to being changed by the efforts of the individual employee in an organization is that
   A. enforcement of unpopular regulations as offended many individuals
   B. the organization itself has an unsatisfactory reputation
   C. the public is not interested in agency matters
   D. there are many errors in judgment committed by individual subordinates

6. It is not enough for an agency's services to be of a high quality; attention must also be given to the acceptability of these services to the general public.
   This statement is GENERALLY
   A. *false*; a superior quality of service automatically wins public support
   B. *true*; the agency cannot generally progress beyond the understanding and support of the public
   C. *false*; the acceptance by the public of agency services determines their quality
   D. *true*; the agency is generally unable to engage in any effective enforcement activity without public support

7. Sustained agency participation in a program sponsored by a community organization is MOST justified when
   A. the achievement of agency objectives in some area depends partly on the activity of this organization
   B. the community organization is attempting to widen the base of participation in all community affairs
   C. the agency is uncertain as to what the community wants
   D. the agency is uncertain as to what the community wants

8. Of the following, the LEAST likely way in which a records system may serve a supervisor is in
   A. developing a sympathetic and cooperative public attitude toward the agency
   B. improving the quality of supervision by permitting a check on the accomplishment of subordinates
   C. permit a precise prediction of the exact incidences in specific categories for the following year
   D. helping to take the guesswork out of the distribution of the agency

9. Assuming that the *grapevine* in any organization is virtually indestructible, the one of the following which it is MOST important for management to understand is:
    A. What is being spread by means of the *grapevine* and the reason for spreading it
    B. What is being spread by means of the *grapevine* and how it is being spread
    C. Who is involved in spreading the information that is on the *grapevine*
    D. Why those who are involved in spreading the information are doing so

10. When the supervisor writes a report concerning an investigation to which he has been assigned, it should be LEAST intended to provide
    A. a permanent official record of relevant information gathered
    B. a summary of case findings limited to facts which tend to indicate the guilt of a suspect
    C. a statement of the facts on which higher authorities may base a corrective or disciplinary action
    D. other investigators with information so that they may continue with other phases of the investigation

11. In survey work, questionnaires rather than interviews are sometimes used. The one of the following which is a DISADVANTAGE of the questionnaire method as compared with the interview is the
    A. difficulty of accurately interpreting the results
    B. problem of maintaining anonymity of the participant
    C. fact that it is relatively uneconomical
    D. requirement of special training for the distribution of questionnaires

12. In his contacts with the public, an employee should attempt to create a good climate of support for his agency.
    This statement is GENERALLY
    A. *false*; such attempts are clearly beyond the scope of his responsibility
    B. *true*; employees of an agency who come in contact with the public have the opportunity to affect public relations
    C. *false*; such activity should be restricted to supervisors trained in public relations techniques
    D. *true*; the future expansion of the agency depends to a great extent on continued public support of the agency

13. The repeated use by a supervisor of a call for volunteers to get a job done is objectionable MAINLY because it
    A. may create a feeling of animosity between the volunteers and the non-volunteers
    B. may indicate that the supervisor is avoiding responsibility for making assignments which will be most productive
    C. is an indication that the supervisor is not familiar with the individual capabilities of his men
    D. is unfair to men who, for valid reasons, do not, or cannot volunteer

14. Of the following statements concerning subordinates' expressions to a supervisor of their opinions and feelings concerning work situations, the one which is MOST correct is that
    A. by listening and responding to such expressions the supervisor encourages the development of complaints
    B. the lack of such expressions should indicate to the supervisor that there is a high level of job satisfaction
    C. the more the supervisor listens to and responds to such expressions, the more he demonstrates lack of supervisory ability
    D. by listening and responding to such expressions, the supervisor will enable many subordinates to understand and solve their own problems on the job

14.____

15. In attempting to motivate employees, rewards are considered preferable to punishment PRIMARILY because
    A. punishment seldom has any effect on human behavior
    B. punishment usually results in decreased production
    C. supervisors find it difficult to punish
    D. rewards are more likely to result in willing cooperation

15.____

16. In an attempt to combat the low morale in his organization, a high level supervisor publicized an *open-door policy* to allow employees who wished to do so to come to him with their complaints.
Which of the following is LEAST likely to account for the fact that no employee came in with a complaint?
    A. Employees are generally reluctant to go over the heads of their immediate supervisor.
    B. The employees did not feel that management would help them.
    C. The low morale was not due to complaints associated with the job.
    D. The employees felt that they had more to lose than to gain.

16.____

17. It is MOST desirable to use written instructions rather than oral instructions for a particular job when
    A. a mistake on the job will not be serious
    B. the job can be completed in a short time
    C. there is no need to explain the job minutely
    D. the job involves many details

17.____

18. If you receive a telephone call regarding a matter which your office does not handle, you should FIRST
    A. give the caller the telephone number of the proper office so that he can dial again
    B. offer to transfer the caller to the proper office
    C. suggest that the caller re-dial since he probably dialed incorrectly
    D. tell the caller he has reached the wrong office and then hang up

18.____

19. When you answer the telephone, the MOST important reason for identifying yourself and your organization is to
    A. give the caller time to collect his or her thoughts
    B. impress the caller with your courtesy
    C. inform the caller that he or she has reached the right number
    D. set a business-like tone at the beginning of the conversation

20. As soon as you pick up the phone, a very angry caller begins immediately to complain about city agencies and *red tape*. He says that he has been shifted to two or three different offices. It turs out that he is seeking information which is not immediately available to you. You believe, you know, however, where it can be found.
    Which of the following actions is the BEST one for you to take?
    A. To eliminate all confusion, suggest that the caller write the agency stating explicitly what he wants.
    B. Apologize by telling the caller how busy city agencies now are, but also tell him directly that you do not have the information he needs.
    C. Ask for the caller's telephone number and assure him you will call back after you have checked further.
    D. Give the caller the name and telephone number of the person who might be able to help, but explain that you are not positive he will get results/

21. Which of the following approaches usually provides the BEST communication in the objectives and values of a new program which is to be introduced?
    A. A general written description of the program by the program manager for review by those who share responsibility
    B. An effective verbal presentation by the program manager to those affected
    C. Development of the plan and operational approach in carrying out the program by the program manager assisted by his key subordinates
    D. Development of the plan by the program manager's supervisor

22. What is the BEST approach for introducing change?
    A
    A. combination of written and also verbal communication to all personnel affected by the change
    B. general bulletin to all personnel
    C. meeting pointing out all the values of the new approach
    D. written directive to key personnel

23. Of the following, committees are BEST used for
    A. advising the head of the organization
    B. improving functional work
    C. making executive decisions
    D. making specific planning decisions

24. An effective discussion leader is one who
    A. announces the problem and his preconceived solution at the start of the discussion
    B. guides and directs the discussion according to pre-arranged outline
    C. interrupts or corrects confused participants to save time
    D. permits anyone to say anything at any time

25. The human relations movement in management theory is basically concerned with
    A. counteracting employee unrest
    B. eliminating the *time and motion* man
    C. interrelationships among individuals in organizations
    D. the psychology of the worker

KEY (CORRECT ANSWERS)

1.	C		11.	A
2.	C		12.	B
3.	A		13.	B
4.	D		14.	D
5.	D		15.	D
6.	B		16.	C
7.	A		17.	D
8.	C		18.	B
9.	A		19.	C
10.	B		20.	C

21.	C
22.	A
23.	A
24.	B
25.	C

EXAMINATION SECTION
TEST 1

DIRECTIONS: Each question or incomplete statement is followed by several suggested answers or completions. Select the one that BEST answers the question or completes the statement. *PRINT THE LETTER OF THE CORRECT ANSWER IN THE SPACE AT THE RIGHT.*

1. Good procedure in handling complaints from the public may be divided into the following four principal stages:
   I. Investigation of the complaint
   II. Receipt of the complaint
   III. Assignment of responsibility for investigation and correction
   IV. Notification of correction

   The ORDER in which these stages ordinarily come is:
   A. III, II, I, IV   B. II, III, I, IV   C. II, III, IV, I   D. II, IV, III, I

   1.____

2. The department may expect the MOST severe public criticism if
   A. it asks for an increase in its annual budget
   B. it purchases new and costly street cleaning equipment
   C. sanitation officers and men are reclassified to higher salary grades
   D. there is delay in cleaning streets of snow

   2.____

3. The MOST important function of public relations in the department should be to
   A. develop cooperation on the part of the public in keeping streets clean
   B. get stricter penalties enacted for health code violations
   C. recruit candidates for entrance positions who ca be developed into supervisors
   D. train career personnel so that they can advance in the department

   3.____

4. The one of the following which has MOST frequently elicited unfavorable public comment has been
   A. dirty sidewalks or streets   B. dumping on lot
   C. failure to curb dogs   D. overflowing garbage cans

   4.____

5. It has been suggested that, as a public relations measure, sections hold *open house* for the public.
   The MOST effective time for this would be
   A. during the summer when children are not in school and can accompany their parents
   B. during the winter when show is likely to fall and the public can see snow removal preparations
   C. immediately after a heavy snow storm when department snow removal operations are in full progress
   D. when street sanitation is receiving general attention as during *Keep City Clean* week

   5.____

6. When a public agency conducts a public relations program, it is MOST likely to find that each recipient of its message will
   A. disagree with the basic purpose of the message if the officials are not well known to him
   B. accept the message if it is presented by someone perceived as having a definite intention to persuade
   C. ignore the message unless it is presented in a literate and clever manner
   D. give greater attention to certain portions of the message as a result of his individual and cultural differences

7. Following are three statements about public relations and communications:
   I. A person who seeks to influence public opinion can speed up a trend
   II. Mass communications is the exposure of a mass audience to an idea
   III. All media are equally effective in reaching opinion leaders
   Which of the following choices CORRECTLY classifies the above statements into those which are correct and those which are not?
   A. I and II are correct, but III is not.
   B. II and III are correct, but I is not.
   C. I and III are correct, but II is not.
   D. III is correct, but I and II are not.

8. Public relations experts say that MAXIMUM effect for a message results from
   A. concentrating in one medium
   B. ignoring mass media and concentrating on *opinion makers*
   C. presenting only those factors which support a given position
   D. using a combination of two or more of the available media

9. To assure credibility and avoid hostility, the public relations man MUST
   A. make certain his message is truthful, not evasive or exaggerated
   B. make sure his message contains some dire consequence if ignored
   C. repeat the message often enough so that it cannot be ignored
   D. try to reach as many people and groups as possible

10. The public relations man MUST be prepared to assume that members of his audience
    A. may have developed attitudes toward his proposals—favorable, neutral, or unfavorable
    B. will be immediately hostile
    C. will consider his proposals with an open mind
    D. will invariably need an introduction to his subject

11. The one of the following statements that is CORRECT is:
    A. When a stupid question is asked of you by the public, it should be disregarded
    B. If you insist on formality between you and the public, the public will not be able to ask stupid questions that cannot be answered
    C. The public should be treated courteously, regardless of how stupid their questions may be
    D. You should explain to the public how stupid their questions are

12. With regard to public relations, the MOST important item which should be emphasized in an employee training program is that
    A. each inspector is a public relations agent
    B. an inspector should give the public all the information it asks for
    C. it is better to make mistakes and give erroneous information than to tell the public that you do not know the correct answer to their problem
    D. public relations is so specialized a field that only persons specially trained in it should consider it

12.____

13. Members of the public frequently ask about departmental procedures. Of the following, it is BEST to
    A. advise the public to put the question in writing so that he can get a proper formal reply
    B. refuse to answer because this is a confidential matter
    C. explain the procedure as briefly as possible
    D. attempt to avoid the issue by discussing other matters

13.____

14. The effectiveness of a public relations program in a public agency such as the authority is BEST indicated by the
    A. amount of mass media publicity favorable to the policies of the authority
    B. morale of those employees who directly serve the patrons of the authority
    C. public's understanding and support of the authority's program and policies
    D. number of complaint received by the authority from patrons using its facilities

14.____

15. In an attempt to improve public opinion about a certain idea, the BEST course of action for an agency to take would be to present the
    A. clearest statements of the idea even though the language is somewhat technical
    B. idea as the result of long-term studies
    C. idea in association with something familiar to most people
    D. idea as the viewpoint of the majority leaders

15.____

16. The fundamental factor in any agency's community relations program is
    A. an outline of the objectives
    B. relations with the media
    C. the everyday actions of the employees
    D. a well-planned supervisory program

16.____

17. The FUNDAMENTAL factor in the success of a community relations program is
    A. true commitment by the community
    B. true commitment by the administration
    C. a well-planned, systematic approach
    D. the actions of individuals in their contacts with the public

17.____

18. The statement below which is LEAST correct is:
    A. Because of selection standards, the supervisor frequently encounters problems resulting from subordinates' inability to express themselves in the language of the profession.
    B. Distortion of the meaning of a communication is usually brought about by a failure to use language that has a precise meaning to others.
    C. The term *filtering* is the distortion or dilution of content of a communication that occurs as information is passed from individual to individual.
    D. The complexity of the *communications net* will directly affect.

19. Consider the following three statements that may or may not be CORRECT:
    I. In order to prevent the stifling of communications flow, supervisors should insist that employees use the formal communications network.
    II. Two-way communications are faster and more accurate than one-way communications.
    III. There is a direct correlation between the effectiveness of communications and the total setting in which they occur.
    The choice below which MOST accurately describes the above statement is:
    A. All three are correct.
    B. All three are incorrect.
    C. More than one statement is correct.
    D. Only one of the statements is correct.

20. The statement below which is MOST inaccurate is:
    A. The supervisor's most important tool in learning whether or not he is communicating well is feedback.
    B. Follow-up is essential if useful feedback is to be obtained.
    C. Subordinates are entitled, as a matter of right, to explanations from management concerning the reasons for orders or directives.
    D. A skilled supervisor is often able to use the grapevine to good advantage.

21. *Since concurrence by those affected is not sought, this kind of communication can be issued with relative ease.*
    The kind of communication being referred to in this quotation is
    A. autocratic   B. democratic   C. directive   D. free-rein

22. The statement below which is LEAST correct is:
    A. Clarity is more important in oral communicating than in written since the readers of a written communication can read it over again.
    B. Excessive use of abbreviations in written communications should be avoided.
    C. Short sentences with simple words are preferred over complex sentences and difficult words in a written communication.
    D. The *newspaper* style of writing ordinarily simplifies expression and facilitates understanding.

23. Which one of the following is the MOST important factor for the department to consider in building a good public image?
    A. A good working relationship with the news media
    B. An efficient community relations program
    C. An efficient system for handling citizen complaints
    D. The proper maintenance of facilities and equipment
    E. The behavior of individuals in their contacts with the public.

24. It has been said that the ability to communicate clearly and concisely is the MOST important single skill of the supervisor.
    Consider the following statements:
    I. The adage, *Actions speak louder than words*, has NO application in superior/subordinate communications since good communications are accomplished with words.
    II. The environment in which a communication takes place will *rarely* determine its effect.
    III. Words are symbolic representations which must be associated with past experience or else they are meaningless.
    The choice below which MOST accurately describes the above statements is:
    A. I, II, and III are correct.
    B. I and II are correct, but III is not.
    C. I and III are correct, but II is not.
    D. III is correct, but I and II are not.
    E. I, II, and III are incorrect.

25. According to expert opinion, the effectiveness of an organization is very dependent upon good upward, downward, and lateral communications. Lateral communications are most important to the activity of coordinating the efforts of organizational units. Before real communication can take place at any level, barriers to communication must be recognized, understood, and removed.
    Consider the following three statements:
    I. The *principal* barrier to good communications is a failure to establish empathy between sender and receiver.
    II. The difference in status or rank between the sender and receiver of a communication may be a communications barrier.
    III. Communications are easier if they travel upward from subordinate to superior
    The choice below which MOST accurately describes the above statements is:
    A. I, II and III are incorrect.   B. I and II are incorrect.
    C. I, II, and III are correct.   D. I and II are correct.
    E. I and III are incorrect.

KEY (CORRECT ANSWERS)

1.	B		11.	C
2.	D		12.	A
3.	A		13.	C
4.	A		14.	C
5.	D		15.	C
6.	D		16.	C
7.	A		17.	D
8.	D		18.	A
9.	A		19.	D
10.	A		20.	C

21. A
22. A
23. E
24. D
25. E

EXAMINATION SECTION

TEST 1

DIRECTIONS: Each question or incomplete statement is followed by several suggested answers or completions. Select the one that BEST answers the question or completes the statement. *PRINT THE LETTER OF THE CORRECT ANSWER IN THE SPACE AT THE RIGHT.*

1. A woman in her mid-30s comes up to your desk and asks you how she can apply to work at your office. You do not know the immediate answer to that question.
   Which of the following would be the BEST way to respond to her request?
   A. Tell her what sounds like the right answer
   B. Tell her to talk to your boss and show her how to do that
   C. Explain you are not allowed to give out confidential information to the public
   D. Inform her that you do not know right now, but you will find out

   1.____

2. A person approaches the customer service desk and asks you to do something that you are ultimately unable to do.
   Which of the following should you avoid doing next?
   A. Opening your policy handbook and reading from it verbatim
   B. Clarifying why you cannot do what he or she is asking of you
   C. Crafting detailed and precise statements
   D. Giving the person alternative options

   2.____

3. When talking to someone from the public, which of the following statements would be LEAST frustrating for the customer to hear?
   A. "You'll have to…" B. "Mr. X will be back at any moment…"
   C. "Let me see what I can do…" D. "I'll do my best…"

   3.____

4. Your office recently received a letter from an individual expressing extreme frustration and disappointment at how it was handling the customer's problems. You have written an apology letter and are reviewing it before sending it to the customer.
   You should ensure the letter is NOT
   A. sincere B. official
   C. personal D. sent immediately

   4.____

5. If you are unable to provide a certain service or product with dependability and accuracy, it would be defined as a lack of
   A. courtesy B. reliability C. assurance D. responsiveness

   5.____

6. As most civil service employees know, customer feedback can be, and usually is, an integral part of customer service.
Which of the following feedback scenarios would be MOST useful to your organization?
    A. When it is an ongoing feedback system
    B. When centered on internal customers
    C. When it is focused on only a few indicators
    D. When every employee can see the feedback coming in

6._____

7. Which of the following is the LEAST important factor in making sure a customer survey is a valuable tool for your company?
    A. Taking every precaution to ensure the survey input is maintained in a confidential manner
    B. Making sure the customers believe in the confidentiality of the survey
    C. Ensuring confidentiality by having an outside company administer the survey
    D. Making sure the employees buy in and promote the survey to customers

7._____

8. Which of the following would NOT be considered part of the resolution process when identifying and dealing with a customers' problems?
    A. Following up with the customer after resolving the issue
    B. Listening and responding to each complaint the customer registers
    C. Giving the customer what they originally requested
    D. Promising the customer whatever you need to

8._____

9. A customer approaches you with a complaint. You want to arrive at a fair solution to the problem.
What is the FIRST step you should take in this situation?
    A. Immediately defend your company from any customer criticisms
    B. Listen to the customer describe their problem
    C. Ask the customer questions to confirm the type of problem they are having
    D. Determine a solution to the customer's problem(s)

9._____

10. If you are dealing with a customer in a prompt manner when addressing their complaints or issues, which of the following are you demonstrating?
    A. Assurance   B. Empathy
    C. Responsiveness   D. Reliability

10._____

11. Steve has recently been hired to work at the postal office in town. A customer comes into the office to complain about the number of packages of his they have lost over the past year.
When Steve attempts to help the upset customer, what should he make sure to do FIRST?
He should
    A. check into how legitimate the customer's complaints are and see if he can do anything about the missing packages
    B. just let the customer blow off some steam and chalk it up to an emotional outburst

11._____

C. ask for help from his boss to see how to handle the situation
D. assume the complaints are accurate and immediately attempt to correct them

12. How should a service representative react when a customer first presents them with a request?
    A. Apologize
    B. Greet them in a friendly manner
    C. Read from the employee handbook about the request
    D. Ask the customer to clarify information

13. In order to assuage a customer's frustration, which of the following should a civil service employee demonstrate?
    A. Compassion   B. Indifference   C. Surprise   D. Agreement

14. A customer comes into the office requesting that your organization do something for them that you know is not part of organization policy.
    Your FIRST responsibility would be to
    A. pass the customer on to higher management to deal with the issue
    B. persuade the customer to believe that the organization can grant their request
    C. mold expectations so they more closely resemble what the organization can do for the customer
    D. tell the customer there is no way you can comply with their request

15. Of the following potential distractors, which one MOST prevents a civil service employee from displaying good listening skills while a customer is speaking?
    A. Cell phones or checking e-mail
    B. Asking superfluous questions
    C. Background office noise
    D. Interrupting the customer to speak with colleagues

16. If you are in a situation where you have to deliver a negative response to a customer, it is often better to say _____ instead of just saying "no"?
    A. "I will try to…"   B. "You can…"
    C. "Our policy does not allow…"   D. "I do not believe…"

17. You are working one-on-one with a customer.
    Which of the following would be the MOST appropriate body language to display?
    A. Make frowning faces
    B. Stare at a spot over the customer's shoulder
    C. Lean in toward the customer
    D. Cross your arms while they speak

18. The majority of communication in face-to-face meetings with customers is shown through
    A. word choice   B. tone
    C. clothing choice   D. body language

19. A customer angrily approaches you at your service desk and starts expressing his frustration with recent actions by your department.
    Which of the following should be your FIRST responses to the customer?
    A. Listen to the person, then express understanding and apologize for how they have been negatively affected by your department's action
    B. Interrupt them while they are speaking and tell them to calm down or you will not help them
    C. Give them an explanation of why your department took the actions they did
    D. None of the above

20. Of the following services, which one is NOT customized to a specific individual's needs?
    A. Hair salon
    B. Elementary education
    C. Computer counseling
    D. Dental care

21. Which of the following civil service employees demonstrates excellent customer service?
    A. A park ranger who minimizes public interaction and contact
    B. The Postal Service employee who sees the customer as a commodity
    C. The office clerk who spends a lot of time with customers sharing personal stories and anecdotes
    D. A DMV employee with open body language and direct communication

22. It is important to have excellent knowledge of services and products, if applicable, when interacting with consumers because
    A. you can demonstrate your knowledge and impress the customer
    B. your organization can have a higher margin of profit regardless of customer benefit
    C. the customer's needs can best be matched with appropriate services/products
    D. you can look good to your superiors and keep your job

23. A park ranger has recently been coming to a kids' camp dirty and unkempt. Even though her job requires her to be outside at ties, why should she still care about her personal appearance?
    A. To speed up her service to the public
    B. So she is seen as a professional in her field
    C. It would help her organizational skills
    D. To show her level of expertise as a park ranger

24. How could guided conversation be a positive with interacting with the public?
    A. It allows you to anticipate a person's needs and expectations.
    B. Most people know what they want even before they show up to your office.
    C. It creates the impression of friendliness.
    D. It helps time move faster.

25. In the event a conflict or crisis arises, which of the following would be considered a POOR action to take when interacting with the public?   25.____
    A. Provide a constant flow of information
    B. Put the public's needs first
    C. Avoid saying "No Comment" as much as possible
    D. Assign multiple spokespeople so media calls can be dealt with efficiently

KEY (CORRECT ANSWERS)

1.	D	11.	A
2.	A	12.	D
3.	C	13.	A
4.	B	14.	C
5.	B	15.	D
6.	A	16.	B
7.	C	17.	C
8.	D	18.	D
9.	B	19.	A
10.	C	20.	B

21.	D
22.	C
23.	B
24.	A
25.	D

TEST 2

DIRECTIONS: Each question or incomplete statement is followed by several suggested answers or completions. Select the one that BEST answers the question or completes the statement. *PRINT THE LETTER OF THE CORRECT ANSWER IN THE SPACE AT THE RIGHT.*

1. John Smith answers a caller who struggles to understand a convoluted policy of your agency.
   How should he handle the customer's question?
   A. Tell the caller to go to the agency's website
   B. He should be honest and say he does not know the answer to the question
   C. John should explain the policy in general terms and refer them to a written version of the policy
   D. Tell the caller to talk to his supervisor and then give the caller the supervisor's extension

   1.____

2. While meeting with a group of young campers at the local parks and recreation office, you conduct a lecture on the importance of avoiding dangerous plants near the forest.
   What can you do to make sure your inexperienced audience remembers the main points of your presentation?
   A. Use flashy visuals that catch the eye
   B. Repeat and emphasize your points
   C. Make jokes so the presentation is livelier
   D. Allow the campers to ask questions at the end of the presentation

   2.____

3. A park ranger is about to deliver a speech at a public conservation meeting.
   Which of the following is the MOST important thing to keep in mind as he preps for the presentation?
   A. How large the audience is
   B. Whether or not he will be able to use visual aids
   C. If he will have time to use charts and graphs
   D. Audience interests

   3.____

4. Jerry receives a letter from a customer and is about to shred it without reading. When you stop him, he says that there is no reason to read it because you cannot learn very much from letters you receive from the public.
   Which of the following should you tell him in order to convince him that reading letters sent from the public is beneficial and necessary?
   A. These public letters can give us a feel for how we are meeting customer needs.
   B. Letters from the public tell us how well our informational efforts are working.
   C. These letters can inform us of what additional training we may need.
   D. The letters can tell us whether public information processes need to be changed or not.

   4.____

5. Ms. Johnson is a volunteer with the Parks and Recreation Department and her children also attend various summer programs through the district. She comes to you today to complain that one of her children was not allowed to join a program because they missed the sign-up by one day. She calls your staff a bunch of "morons" and complains that your department's actions are creating serious issues for her.
   How should you handle this situation?
   A. Let Ms. Johnson rant until she gets it out of her system
   B. Tell her you cannot help her and will ask her to leave if she cannot stop referring to your colleagues as "morons"
   C. Refer Ms. Johnson to your boss
   D. Try to alter the tone of the conversation to a more objective and less emotional discussion of Ms. Johnson's problems

5.____

6. A civil service employee is tasked with moderating a town hall meeting regarding child safety, but he knows that residents will be attending the meeting with different motives.
   How can the employee make sure the town hall meeting is as beneficial and informational as possible?
   A. Ask attendees to be open to changing their opinions and preferences
   B. Start out by recognizing the various motives but also stress the common objectives and interests
   C. Call out individuals who you know have specific reasons for attending and put them on the spot
   D. Cancel the meeting and avoid rescheduling it until you can be sure everyone is on the same page

6.____

7. During the question-and-answer session at the end of a presentation, a member of the public makes a suggestion that you deem not only practical but worthy of further discussion.
   How should you react to this?
   A. Tell them you will let the appropriate people know of the suggestion
   B. Tell the person you concur with them wholeheartedly
   C. Let the person know you think it is a good idea but you cannot make decisions based on suggestions during Q and A
   D. Even though the suggestion is good, tell the person that someone in your organization has probably already thought of the idea

7.____

8. When in a conversation with a group of local residents, what is the BIGGEST problem with one or two people dominating the conversation?
   A. Your interaction could take longer than it should
   B. Some people will become distracted and not focus on the meeting anymore
   C. The other member of the group may not have an opportunity to share their opinions
   D. None of the above

8.____

9. You receive a phone call at the village hall, but the information being requested would need to come from the police station.
   How should you respond to the caller?
   A. Give them the police station's website and wish them well
   B. Tell them you are not responsible for their request
   C. Refer them to the police station's number and information
   D. Provide them with the information as best as you can

10. Which of the following should almost always be avoided when interacting with a member of the community?
    A. Contentious matters
    B. Topics about financial material
    C. Rules and regulations
    D. Technical lingo or jargon

11. When people use inflammatory language laced with obscenities, a town employee should
    A. refuse to continue the dialogue if the person cannot stop using the offensive language
    B. tell the person to talk to your supervisor
    C. allow the person to finish "venting" before attempting to find a solution to the problem
    D. hang up if on the phone; if in person, leave the area and ask the individual to leave as well

12. A member of the public has sent your agency a letter.
    Which of the following will help you figure out how much explaining you need to do when writing a response?
    A. Go to the agency website and search for how much explanation is provided there
    B. Take out the original customer letter and study it
    C. Presume the person who wrote the letter already has a working knowledge of the subject and thus will not require a lot of background explanation
    D. Look at past letters sent by your agency

13. During an informational meeting with local townspeople, a man makes a suggestion for a new town measure that is based on incorrect information and is impractical.
    What is the BEST way to handle a situation such as this?
    A. Ask if anyone else in attendance would like to respond to the suggestion
    B. Tell the person it is a great idea even though you are aware of its folly
    C. Thank the man for coming and tell everyone you always welcome their suggestions
    D. Inform the person that his/her comment clearly reflects an inferior knowledge about the subject

14. A member from the public calls your office about negative comments he has heard about one of your programs. You believe the comments were made by someone who had inaccurate material, but you are not completely certain of that because you are not directly involved with the program.

What is the BEST way to handle this situation?
- A. Tell the caller you will analyze the situation in depth and then call them back
- B. Tell the caller the evidence on which they have based their judgment is not supported
- C. Explain that your office has a "No Comment" policy regarding negative comments
- D. Let the caller know you are not involved with the program directly, and tell them to call the person who is

15. Which of the following quotes reflects the BEST way to handle an angry resident that keeps interrupting during a village meeting?
    - A. "I am here as a volunteer and I do not need this."
    - B. "I understand your anger, but we have quite a bit of information to cover tonight, so in fairness to everyone else, please let me continue."
    - C. "Every crowd has one black sheep in it."
    - D. "Sir, (or Ma'am) if you cannot stop interjecting, I will have security escort you from the premises."

16. Of the following, which is an example of nonverbal communication?
    - A. Frowning
    - B. Hand signs
    - C. A "21 Gun Salute"
    - D. All of the above

17. Residents of Masterton, Georgia, were recently made aware that the main road into and out of town will be under construction for the next four years. The construction will make travel time much more difficult for the citizens and they have demanded a meeting with your department. You are tasked with creating a presentation to explain to them why the construction is necessary.
    At the start of the presentation, you should
    - A. make a joke to lighten the mood
    - B. state the purpose of your presentation
    - C. provide a detailed account of the history behind the project
    - D. make a call to action

18. When a member of the public asks questions that are confusing or you do not understand right away, what is the BEST way to handle this situation?
    - A. Answer the question as you understand it
    - B. Stick to generalizations dealing with the subject of the question
    - C. Rephrase the question and ask the person if you understood what they were asking
    - D. Ask the person to repeat the question

19. When preparing for a public interaction, which of the following situations would be MOST appropriate to include handouts?
    - A. If you want to help the attendees remember important information after the interaction is over
    - B. If you want to keep the interaction short

C. When you want to remember key points to talk about
D. When you do not want attendees to have to pay attention during the interaction

20. John is in the process of handling a phone call when a local citizen approaches his desk to ask a question. Neither the caller nor the visitor seem to be in a crisis.
What should John do in this scenario?
    A. Keep talking with the caller until he is finished. Then tell the visitor he is sorry for making them wait.
    B. Remain on the phone with the caller but look up at the visitor every once and awhile so they know he has not forgotten about them.
    C. Tell the caller he has a visitor, so the conversation needs to end.
    D. Tell the visitor he will be with them as soon as he finishes the phone call.

21. When engaged in conversation with another person, which communication technique is MOST likely to ensure you comprehend fully what the other person to trying to communicate to you?
    A. Repeat back to the person what you think they are communicating
    B. Continual eye contact
    C. Making sure the person speaks slowly
    D. Nodding your head while they speak

22. You encounter someone who is frustrated about a situation and needs to vent by talking it out before they can move onto a productive conversation.
When a situation is like this, it is often BEST to
    A. recommend various strategies for calming down
    B. Ask to be excused from the conversation without offering why
    C. Explain to the person that it is unproductive to behave the way they are currently behaving
    D. Acknowledge that venting is a crucial step to moving past the emotions and allow the person to express his or her feelings

23. Which of the following is NOT an example of active listening?
    A. Taking notes
    B. Referring the customer to the manager after they are done speaking
    C. Using phrases like "I see" or "Go on"
    D. Repeating back to the customer what you've heard

24. Which of the following questions would be classified as a clarification question?
    A. "How long have you sold spoiled meat?"
    B. "Do you like our brand?"
    C. "You mentioned you liked this merchandise. How would you feel about this?"
    D. None of the above

25. When interacting with a member of the public, which of the following words should you avoid using as it is not positive as perceived by most people? 25._____
    A. "Absolutely" B. "You are welcome"
    C. "Here's what I can do" D. "I'll do my best"

KEY (CORRECT ANSWERS)

1. C
2. B
3. D
4. A
5. D

6. B
7. A
8. C
9. C
10. D

11. A
12. B
13. C
14. A
15. B

16. D
17. B
18. C
19. A
20. D

21. A
22. D
23. B
24. C
25. D

BASIC FUNDAMENTALS OF INTERPERSONAL RELATIONSHIPS

TABLE OF CONTENTS

	Page
INSTRUCTIONAL OBJECTIVES	1
CONTENT	1
INTRODUCTION	1
1. Interpersonal Conduct and Behavior on the Job	1
Formal Organization of the Office	2
Office as a Setting for Formal and Informal Relations	2
Office Behavior	2
2. Interpersonal Communication – The Meaning	3
Importance of Face-to-Face Contacts	3
Listening Techniques	3
3. Factors in Interpersonal Communication	3
The Choice of Words of the Conversant	4
How Each Sees Each Other	4
The Right Time and Place	4
The Effect of Past Experience	4
The Effect of Personal Differences	5
4. Defense Mechanisms in Interpersonal Relations	5
Causes for Defense Mechanisms	5
Results of Use of Defense Mechanisms	5
5. Influences of Role Playing in Interpersonal Relations	6
Exploring Superior-Subordinate Relations	6
Interpersonal Relations Achieved Through Simulation	7
6. Measuring Interpersonal Relations	7
Survey of Interpersonal Values	7
Analysis of Interpersonal Behavior	8
STUDENT LEARNING ACTIVITIES	8
TEACHER MANAGEMENT ACTIVITIES	9
EVALUATION QUESTIONS	10

BASIC FUNDAMENTALS OF INTERPERSONAL RELATIONSHIPS

INSTRUCTIONAL OBJECTIVES

1. Ability to distinguish between formal and informal behavior.
2. Ability to identify the important factors in communicating with people.
3. Ability to understand how defense mechanisms affect communication with others.
4. Ability to identify the roles played in effective person-to-person communication.
5. Ability to acquire the human relations skills needed for getting along with others both on and off the job.
6. Ability to establish greater personal effectiveness with others so as to develop better cooperation and superior-subordinate relationships in public-service working situations.
7. Ability to recognize the mutual dependence of individuals on each other.
8. Ability to form positive attitudes toward the worth and dignity of every human being.
9. Ability to become aware of how feelings affect one's own behavior, as well as one's relationships with other people.
10. Ability to use an understanding of human relationships to effectively work with people.
11. Ability to improve communications with others by developing greater effectiveness in dealing with people in the world of public service.

CONTENT

INTRODUCTION

Perhaps the single most important skill that a public-service worker, or anyone for that matter, needs, is the ability to get along with other people. "Person-to-person" relationships are the building blocks of all social interactions between two-individuals. If there is one essential ingredient for success in life, both on and off the job, it is developing greater effectiveness in dealing with people.

The skill of the teacher is critical to the success of this unit. He should establish a permissive and non-threatening group climate in which free communication and behavior can take place. The importance of this unit cannot be over stated. The overall objective is to establish greater personal effectiveness with others and to develop better co-operative and superior-subordinate relationships in the public-service occupations. Obtaining greater "self-awareness" is a large part of this goal. Because interpersonal relations are affected by a variety of factors, some attention should be given initially to basic rules of conduct and behavior on the job.

1. ### INTERPERSONAL CONDUCT AND BEHAVIOR ON THE JOB
   Most public-service agencies have clearly defined rules and regulations. The behavior of the public-service worker is often guided by the established proce-

dures and directives of that individual agency. In many cases, even individual departments or units will have procedures manuals, which regulate conduct and office work.

Formal Organization of the Office

At one point or another, most public-service employees either work directly in an office, or come in frequent contact with other people working in an administrative or staff office. Students should become familiar with the organizational structure of the occupational groups in which they are planning on working. A park worker, for example, must know about the organization of the Parks Department—what kinds of staff or administrative services are provided, what about training, what are the safety rules, what goes into personnel records, etc. Preparing a flow chart of the relationships between different positions in a particular agency is one way of learning about the organization of that office or agency.

Office as a Setting for formal and Informal Relations

It is necessary to become aware of the different kinds of social relations shared with co-workers and the public. Some co-workers, for example, are seen only at work, and others are seen socially after work and/or on weekends. Factors that determine which co-workers become *personal* friends and which are just *work* friends should be considered and discussed.

On the other hand, a public-service worker usually has more formal relationships with the public with whom he comes into contact. Consider the relationships of the preschool teacher's aide and his students, the library helper and his library patrons, the police cadet and the general public, etc. In each of these cases, the public expects the public-service worker to help them with a particular service.

Although the distinction between formal and informal social relationships is not always clear, one should be sensitive to the fact that both kinds of relationships affect the behavior of the public and the public-service employee, Normally, the very organization of the public-service office helps to create a social climate for developing working relationships of a formal nature, and personal relationships with co-workers and the public which are of a more impersonal nature.

Office Behavior

Specific kinds of behavior relate to these formal and informal relationships with other people. Typically, the formal relationship is well prescribed and regulated by procedures or directives. The license interviewer, as an example, has specific questions to ask, and specific information to obtain from the applicant. Their relationship can be described as formal or prescribed by regulation. On the other hand, other office behavior can best be described as informal and non-prescribed (or *free*). Interpersonal relations in this case are often more personal and relaxed by their very nature.

2. INTERPERSONAL COMMUNICATION - THE MEANING

   Interpersonal communication can be defined as a two-way flow of information from person-to-person. One cannot Study human relations without examining the constant relationships that man has with other people; the individual does not exist in a vacuum. Most of man's psychological and social needs are met through dealings with other people. In fact, one psychiatrist (Harry Stark Sullivan) has developed a theory of personality based upon interpersonal situations. This viewpoint, known as the *Interpersonal Theory of Psychiatry,* claims that personality is essentially the enduring pattern of continued interpersonal relationships between people. This interpersonal behavior is all that can be observed as personality.

   Importance of Face-to-Face Contacts

   The very phrase. *Public Service Occupations,* suggests frequent face-to-face contacts with not only the general public, but with co-workers as well. With possibly a few exceptions, practically every public-service employee encounters frequent person-to-person contacts both on and off the job. The ability to get along with people is a very important part of public-service work.

   Listening Techniques

   Effective listening is a critical part of interpersonal communications. Listening is an active process, requiring not only that one must *pay attention* to what is being said, but that one must also *listen* for the meaning of what is being said. Almost one-half of the total time spent communicating, (reading, writing, speaking, or listening) is spent in listening.

   Even though people get considerable practice at listening, they don't do too well at it. Many studies have shown that, on the average, a person retains only about 25 percent of a given speech after only 10 minutes have elapsed. Most people forget three quarters of what they hear in a relatively short period of time. Clearly, people need to improve their listening skills if they are to become more effective in their relations with other people.

3. FACTORS IN INTERPERSONAL COMMUNICATION
   There are a number of components that affect the person-to-person relationship. Some of the factors common to both the sender and the receiver in a person-to-person communication are:

   The Attitudes and Emotions of the Individuals

   > For example - two people are shouting and screaming at each other - how effective is their interpersonal communication?

   ◦ *The Needs and Wants of the People Communicating*

Both the sender and receiver have unique desires, some open, and some hidden from the other person. These needs can and do strongly influence interpersonal relationships.

- *The Implied Demands of the Sender and Receiver*

    An important factor in interpersonal communications involves requests or demands. How are these demands handled? What are some typical responses to demands? These factors are common to both the sender and the receiver in interpersonal relations and affect the individual behavior of the people communicating.

The Choice of Words of the Conversant

One's choice of words can have a direct bearing on the interpersonal communication. The vocabulary one uses in interpersonal relationships should be appropriate for the occasion. For example, a preschool teacher's aide would not use the same vocabulary in talking to a three-year-old, as she would in talking to the preschool teacher.

How Each Sees the Other

The process of communicating from person-to-person is greatly influenced by the perception that the sender and receiver have of each other. The feelings that a person has toward the other person are reflected in his tone of voice, choice of words, and even in his *body language*. A reference book mentioned in the resource section of this unit, *How to Read a Person Like a Book,* deals with the importance of body language in person-to-person relationships.

The Right Time and Place

Another factor that may be important in interpersonal relationships is the timing of the communication. For example, one of the first things a supervisor should do if he wants to talk over a problem with his subordinate, is ask the question: "Is this the right time and place?" Problems should not generally be discussed in the middle of an office, where other employees, or the public, can hear the discussion. Personal problems should be discussed only in private.

The Effect of Past Experience

In general, the quality of the person-to-person transaction will depend upon the past experience of the individuals. Human beings have acquired most of their opinions, assumptions, and value judgments through their relationships with other people. Past experience not only helps to teach people about effective interpersonal relationships, it is also often responsible for the irrational prejudices that a person displays. A strong bias usually blocks the interpersonal relationship if the subject of the communication concerns that particular bias.

The Effect of Personal Differences

An additional factor in interpersonal communications involves the intelligence and other personal differences of the people communicating. An example of such a personal difference is the *objectivity* of the people involved, as compared with their *subjectivity*. One person may try to be very fair and objective in discussing a point with another person, yet this other person is, at the same time, taking everything personally and being very subjective in his viewpoint. It is almost as if an adult was talking to an angry child.

Such differences can impede the communications flow between two people. In fact, all the factors mentioned in communications should be examined as to whether they block or facilitate interpersonal relationships. *The most effective interpersonal relationships are those that are adult-like in their character.*

4. DEFENSE MECHANISMS IN INTERPERSONAL RELATIONS

   Defense mechanisms are attempts to defend the individual from anxiety. They are essentially a reaction to frustration - a self-deception.

   ## Causes for Defense Mechanisms

   In order to help understand some of the causes for defense mechanisms, remember the basic human needs:

   - *Biological or physiological needs* - hunger, water, rest, etc.
   - *Psychological or social needs* - status, security, affection, justice etc.

   Fear of failure in any of these basic needs appears to be related to the development of defense mechanisms; attitudes toward failure, in turn, originate out of the fabric of childhood experience. The social and cultural conditions encountered during childhood determine the rewards and controls which fill one's later life. These childhood experiences, and their resultant consequences, affect personality development, the individual's value system, and his definition of acceptable goals.

   Individuals who are dominated by the fear of failure may react by using one of these defense mechanisms:

   - *Rationalization* - making an impulsive action seem logical.

   - *Projection* - assigning one's traits to others.

   - *Identification* - assuming someone else's favorite qualities are their own.

   ## Results of Use of Defense Mechanisms

   A common factor to all defense mechanisms is their quality of *self-deception*. People cling to their impulses and actions, perhaps disguising them so that they become socially acceptable. Their defense mechanisms can be found in the everyday behavior of most normal people and, of course, have *direct influences* on interpersonal relationships.

A person, for example, who is responsible for a particular job makes a mistake, and the work doesn't get done. When confronted with the problem by his supervisor, the individual puts the blame on someone or something else. This is a very common form of a defense mechanism.

Defense mechanisms can sometimes have *negative influences* on interpersonal communications. They can contribute to the individual forming erroneous opinions about the other person's motives. These mechanisms can alter the perceptions and evaluations made about the individual by other people, Ways to understand these mechanisms must be sought; one solution is to become more aware of the common defense mechanisms, and to become less defensive through greater acceptance of others.

5. THE INFLUENCES OF ROLE-PLAYING IN INTERPERSONAL RELATIONS

Everyone wears a mask and plays a certain role or roles in life. Even if the role one plays is to be himself, that particular form of behavior can still be considered a role. As a public-service employee, one's role is to serve the public. This can be done in a number of ways. Some of the factors involved in public-service roles will be mentioned below:

Exploring Superior-Subordinate Relations

Public-service employees are accountable for their actions. From the entry-level public administrative analysis trainee, to the President of the United States, every public servant must be accountable to either an immediate supervisor, a governing body, or to the public itself. Entry-level public-service employees gain experience and get promoted, but they continue to be subordinates and responsible for their actions, even though they also become supervisors and have people working for them.

Simulation exercises can be developed which will examine the perceptions of the superior by the subordinate. *Authority* and *power* factors may enter in here, as the superior also perceives the subordinate in a particular way. *Dominance* and *need* factors are at work in superior-subordinate relationships, and the style of leadership used *(autocratic, democratic,* or *lassiez-faire)* is a form of leadership role.

Peer relationships can be explored through simulation exercises. The ways in which co-workers perceive each other and the resultant effect on cooperation is one area to be examined. Ways to establish a climate or environment for effective, cooperative relations should be sought.

It is desirable also to simulate, for better comprehension, interpersonal communications with the general public. Role-playing techniques, which permit the exploration of person-to-person relationships, are highlighted in the following section on simulation exercises.

Interpersonal Relations Achieved Through Simulation

The preparation of students for entry-level public-service occupations must include an opportunity to experience meaningful interpersonal relations. Public-service employees, whether office or field workers, experience personal relationships with other people every day. The initial success of the public-service worker will depend in large measure upon his ability to interact effectively with others in the office or field. Accordingly, a principle objective of simulation exercises for entry-level public-service education is to have the student acquire the necessary interpersonal relations skills that make for success in all public-service occupations.

When developing a model public-service simulation with the principal objective being to improve favorable interpersonal relations, certain criteria must be established. These criteria may be stated as follows:

- *Interpersonal relations must be the principal component of the simulation.* Provision must be made for students to interact with others in an office interpersonal setting so that they may work and communicate effectively with one another.

- *The simulation must be as realistic as possible.* Realism can best be accomplished by simulating an actual public-service operation in as many areas as possible.

- *Originality must play an important part.* Model simulations, currently in use, must not be copied in an effort to maintain simplicity.

- *The simulation must be interesting.* Students must be motivated to participate in the simulation and to be enthusiastic about its operation.

- *The simulation must be unstructured.* Provision must be made to allow for an awareness of events as they take place. Students must learn to cope with a situation without prior knowledge that the situation will occur.

In order for the teacher to determine if the model public-service simulation developed has, in fact, improved interpersonal relations, the simulation must be evaluated in terms of meeting the established objectives.

6. ## MEASURING INTERPERSONAL RELATIONS
Survey of Interpersonal Values

A valid and reliable instrument for measuring interpersonal relations, such as the *Survey of Interpersonal Values,* may be used for this purpose. This instrument is intended for grades 9-12, and is designed to measure the relative importance of the major factored interpersonal value dimensions. These values include both the subject's relations with others and others with himself. The value dimensions considered are:

- *Support*--being treated with understanding, encouragement, kindness, and consideration.

- *Conformity*--doing what is socially correct, accepted, and proper.

- *Recognition*--being admired, looked up to, considered important, and attracting favorable notice.

- *Independence*--being able to do what one wants to do, making one's own decisions, doing things in one's own way.

- *Benevolence*--doing things for other people, sharing, and helping.

- *Leadership*--being in charge of others, having authority or power.

A pretest on interpersonal values is administered before the model public-service simulation actually begins, and the same test is administerd as a post-test after a stipulated period of time. By comparison of results, and through the use of applicable statistics, the gain in behavior modification in interpersonal relations can be determined, as a result of using the model public-service simulation.

Analysis of Interpersonal Behavior

Public-service employees should be aware of their own needs, and of the needs of other people. They should be able to recognize situations or behavior calling for professional help, and be able to refer people to such appropriate help. New employees must be able to use their knowledge of person-to-person relationships to effectively work with people.

In order to become more effective in interpersonal relationships, students must gain an understanding of:

- *Self-evaluation* - to be able to assess their own strengths and weaknesses.

- *Group Evaluation* - as a class to be able to evaluate other individuals' competencies in interpersonal communications.

- *Correction of own self-perception* - to be able to do something about the knowledge and attitudes formed by adjusting their individual behavior.

STUDENT LEARNING ACTIVITIES

- Define formal and informal social behavior.

- List the important factors in interpersonal communication.

- View and discuss the film strip, *Your Educational Goals, No. 2: Human Relationships.*

- Role play in alternate supervisor-subordinate relationships practicing effective interpersonal communication.

- Write an essay on "Defense mechanisms affect interpersonal relationships."

- View the film, *The Unanswered Question,* and discuss human relationships afterwards.

- Listen to a discussion of structured interpersonal communications and evaluate the effectiveness of the person-to-person relationship.

- In small groups, discuss the ways in which people are mutually dependent on each other,
- Use simulation exercises to practice interpersonal relations.
- List the different kinds of roles and games played in interpersonal communications.
- Debate the statement: *Understanding person-to-person relations is one of the most important skills a person can acquire for success in life.*
- Discuss how understanding interpersonal relationships can help a person to effectively work with people.
- Define the role of recognizing one's own feelings in relation to others.

TEACHER MANAGEMENT ACTIVITIES

- Have the students define formal and informal social behavior.
- Show transparencies on interpersonal relations, *(Social Sensitivity lour Relationship with Others)* and discuss concepts afterwards.
- Assign written exercises on the important factors in interpersonal communication.
- Set up role-playing exercises on subordinate-supervisor roles in effective interpersonal communication.
- Encourage small-group discussions of the ways people are mutually dependent on each other.
- Show a movie on human relationships *(The Unanswered Question)* and discuss key points afterwards.
- Separate the class into teams to debate such statements as: Understanding interpersonal relations is one of the most important skills a person can acquire for success in life.
- Encourage individual study and reading in interpersonal relationships.
- Assign an essay on the worth and dignity of man in interpersonal relations.
- Bring in public-service workers who deal with others to talk to the class about the value of effective interpersonal communications.

Evaluation Questions

Fill in the crossword puzzle below.

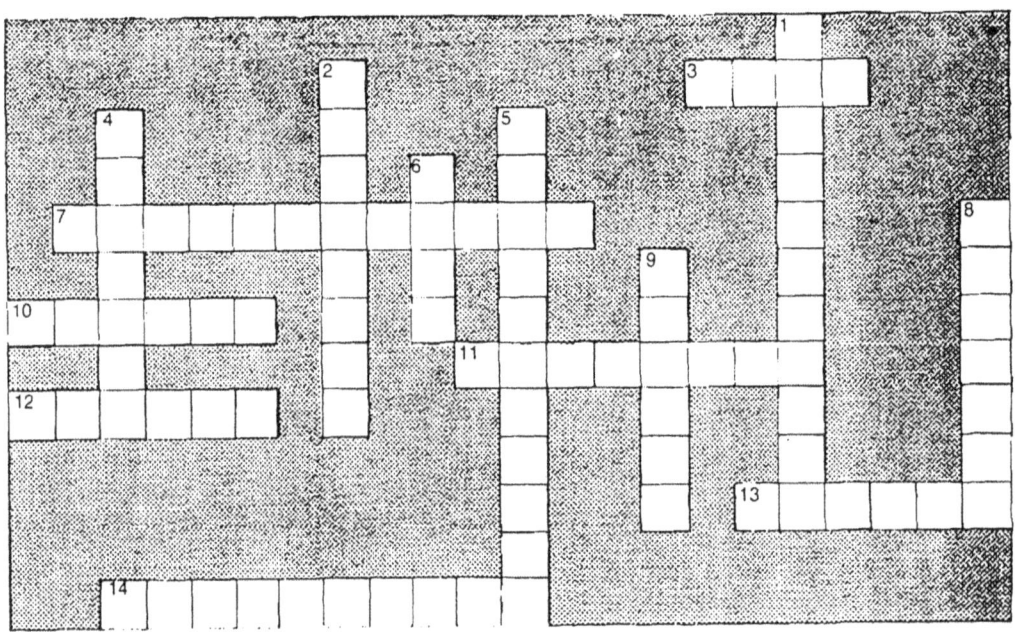

ACROSS:
3. A strong prejudice or _____ can block good relationships.
7. Being able to do what one wants to do satisfies the need for _____.
10. One's _____ of words should be correct for the occasion.
11. Friends usually have an _____ relationship.
12. In talking over problems with others, is important.
13. Everyone needs to feel _____.
14. _____ is assigning one's traits to others.

DOWN:
1. We _____ when we try to make our actions seem logical.
2. When we assume someone's qualities as our own we _____ with that person.
4. Individuals _____ when they do what is socially proper.
5. When we attract favorable attention, we gain _____
6. Some people have a strong _____ of failure.
8. _____ mechanics help to protect a person from anxiety.
9. A public service worker usually has a _____ relationship with the public.

Answer Key

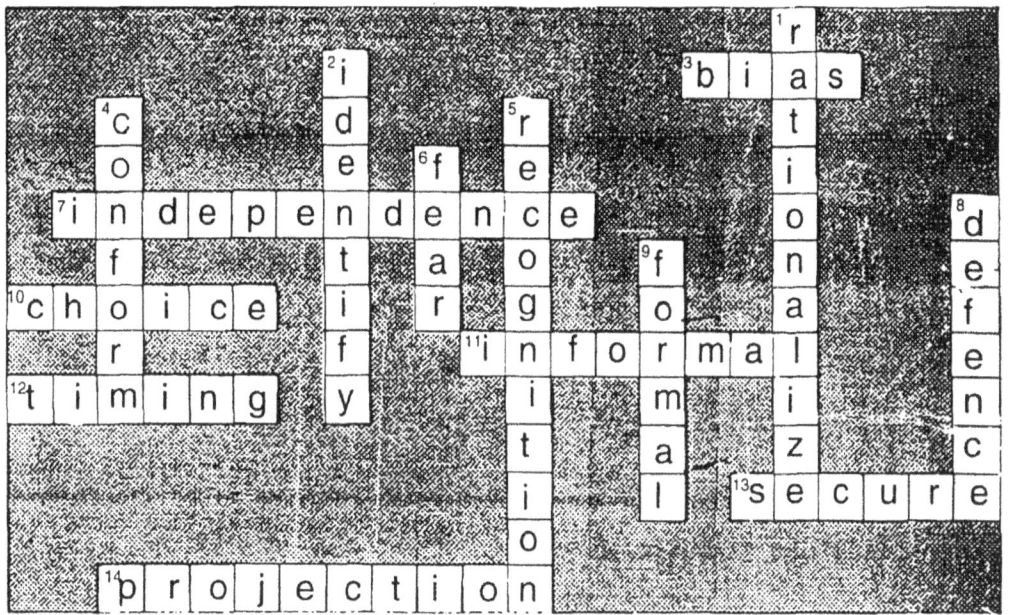

www.ingramcontent.com/pod-product-compliance
Lightning Source LLC
Chambersburg PA
CBHW082126230426
43671CB00015B/2823